PRAYING THROUGH THE SEVEN CHURCHES OF REVELATION AND BEYOND

DAN R. CRAWFORD

Copyright © 2021, Dan R. Crawford

All rights reserved.

No part of this publication may be reproduced or transmitted in any form or by any means, electronic or mechanical, including photocopying and recording, or by any information storage and retrieval system, except in the case of brief quotations for use in articles and reviews, without written permission from the copyright owner.

The views expressed in the book are the author's and do not necessarily reflect those of the publisher.

Portions of this book were published earlier as a part of the author's earlier book, *The Prayer-Shaped Disciple*, Hendrickson Publishers, Inc. Peabody, Massachusetts, 1999 and are used here by permission.

Unless otherwise noted, all Scripture quotations are taken from the New King James Version of the Bible, (c) 1979, 1980, 1982 by Thomas Nelson Inc., Publishers. Used by permission.

7710-T Cherry Park Dr, Ste 224
Houston, TX 77095
www.WorldwidePublishingGroup.com
(713) 766-4271

Cover design: http://HarvestCreek.net

CONTENTS

What Others Are Saying	v
Dedication	1
Preface	3
Introduction: Letters to the Seven Churches	5
1. The Church at Ephesus and Beyond	21
2. The Church at Smyrna and Beyond	33
3. The Church at Pergamos and Beyond	47
4. The Church at Thyatira and Beyond	57
5. The Church at Sardis and Beyond	69
6. The Church at Philadelphia and Beyond	79
7. The Church at Laodicea and Beyond	91
Conclusion	103
Appendix A: How to Get to Heaven from Asia Minor	105
Bibliography	107

WHAT OTHERS ARE SAYING

"Brilliantly insightful and astonishingly practical! Dan's lifetime of prayer, education, and experience brings the wisdom and warnings of the seven churches to life and our lives while leading us in battle against these same trials and temptations we must fight with fervent prayer and faith as the Church today."
   -- **Kathy Branzell**, President, National Day of Prayer Task Force

"The first time I saw Dr. Crawford preaching through the "Seven Churches" series was when I viewed a streaming video captured when he was serving as Interim Pastor at another church. Then, when he was serving my church, I encouraged him to share the series with my church family. He agreed to do so. Our church benefited greatly from the series. Now Dr. Crawford has incorporated that series into book form, and it is available to anyone who desires to learn from the Revelation churches and be inspired to be more and do more as praying Christians."
   -- **Gerre Joiner**, Minister for Senior Adults, First Baptist Church, Decatur, Texas

"Dan Crawford has a unique ability to bring the truths of the Bible to life in magnificent color and beautiful application for today. In Praying

Through the Seven Churches of Revelation and Beyond, he leads his readers to a clearer understanding of the Seven Churches and the messages given to each along with applications for today. The true blessing of each chapter is the prayer prompts at the end that will lead the reader to lift today's churches considering the lessons learned from the Seven Churches. Nothing is more important for the Church today than the prayers of the saints."

-- **Dr. Lisa Seeley**, Director of the Great Commission Center and Global Education, East Texas Baptist University

"I was privileged to accompany Dr. Crawford to the sites of those seven churches on that initial trip in 2000. I experienced his teaching which brought those churches to life. In additional research for this work, he greatly adds to our understanding. I especially like the expansion of the simple mention of Jezebel at Thyatira and the financial conditions at Laodicea."

-- **Dr. Robert McEachern**, missionary to Korea, and "Personalization Networking Team Strategist," International Mission Board (Retired).

"Praying Through the Seven Churches of Revelation and Beyond gave me a richer and clearer understanding of the seven churches of Revelation; each message and church sprang to life. Dr. Crawford shows how each message can apply to today's churches and the Christian community in general. The 'Prayer Prompters' make each message personal. I will use this in my future Bible studies; I'll never again look at the seven churches in the same way."

-- **Glennda Cook**, International Mission Board, Taiwan

"Have you traveled to the seven churches of the book of Revelation? Thought about it? What if you could tour the area with someone who has been there and knows not only the lay of the land but also the relationship of that land to your church? Dr. Crawford allows us to go there without traveling there. Whether you have been there, plan to go there, or never expect to go there, 'Praying through the Seven Churches of Revelation and Beyond' will take you there and show you how to pray from there back to your church."

-- **Dennis Fuqua**, President, International Renewal Ministries, Vancouver, Washington

"In this book Dr. Crawford walks the reader through the archeological ruins of what were formerly thriving first century outposts of the Christian faith in Asia Minor. The Seven Churches of Revelation received praise and critique from the Holy Spirit, and these are points of interaction for our own prayer lives. You will enjoy his insight and humor, even as you appreciate the wisdom with which he guides your heart and mind. We have seen most of these cities and wish that the church still thrived there. To have the opportunity to translate these insights from Revelation and pray them into our own churches--is a valuable treasure."

-- **Tom & Bonnie Hearon**, Former IMB missionaries to Brazil & Europe; stateside missionaries with Global Gates Network.

"Embarking on the journey of *Praying through the Seven Churches of Revelation and Beyond* is a must read for those interested in the early church. The book opens one's eyes and heart to the early church, their victories and challenges and the inclusion of the prayer emphasis is a tremendous plus for the reader. The reader will be rewarded as they study and pray through the 'Seven Churches of Revelation and Beyond.'"

-- **Sonny Sweatman**, IMB Missionary to Eastern & Southern Africa and then Missional Church Strategist for the International Mission Board (Retired).

"This book gives me an opportunity to remember the wonderful trip to Turkey and the visit to the seven churches."

-- **Bonnie J. Wiggs**, missionary to South Korea, International Mission Board (Retired).

"I was blessed to hear Dan Crawford preach this series at a church in transition where I served. I remember the challenge these great truths of scripture posed then and have used the notes from this series as a guide to preach to my current congregation. Dan's additional work and insight offered in this book present both a challenge and an opportunity for a guided introspection and evaluation of the heart and ministry of any church. A prayerful reading will leave you well prepared to '...hear what the Spirit says to the churches.'"

-- **John C. Cullison**, Pastor, First Baptist Church of Geronimo, Oklahoma.

"With an incredible blend of historical accuracy and spiritual insight, Dr. Dan Crawford brings the seven churches of Revelation into a contemporary context for the Church today. After almost 30 years of prayer ministry in local churches, I especially appreciated the very practical blessing of guiding readers into scripture-based prayer. May we, the Church, hear what the Spirit is saying as God speaks to us through this powerful resource."

-- **Kim Butts**, Co-founder and Vice President, Harvest Prayer Ministries.

DEDICATION

To the two churches where I served as pastor and the more than twenty-five churches where I served as Interim Pastor, while I was on the faculty of Southwestern Baptist Seminary in Fort Worth, Texas.

PREFACE

The invitation was most unusual. It came from the International Mission Board and involved a teaching challenge with a group of their employees and missionaries. The idea was to tour the sites of the seven churches of Asia Minor addressed by John in the Book of Revelation. I was to teach about the background of each church and the contents of the letter to each, but there was more. After my teaching, the group was to depart the tour bus, and prayer-walk the site, applying lessons learned from my teaching to their own church, and churches with which they were familiar.

Always one for a challenge, I accepted and blocked the dates on my calendar. As the dates of the tour approached, a major earthquake hit parts of Turkey where we were to travel, thus, postponing our tour for several months. This was a welcome delay, giving me additional time to prepare.

One surprise to me was the fact that the government of Turkey required a trained tour guide to accompany each group and lecture on the sites visited. So the pattern was established, the tour guide would present a rather formal, well researched, and rather secular lecture on the site, followed by my rather informal, more personal and more spiritual sharing of my notes. The only spiritual aspect of the tour guide's presentation was an orange and black covered, paperback version of *Good News for Modern Man*, from which she read the accounts in Revelation.

I noticed that the tour guide was extremely attentive when I shared. Following the tour, she asked me where I found all my information, and could I possibly send her a copy of my notes. I gladly did so, with an addition to each church site, entitled "How to Get to Heaven from Ephesus," "How to Get to Heaven from Smyrna," Etc. This of course was an applied version of the plan of salvation. Since, I never heard from her again, I'm not sure if she understood this portion of my notes, or if she shared this with her future tour groups. The possibility was worth the effort. In Appendix A of this book, I have adapted these additions of my lecture notes into one presentation, entitled, "How to Get to Heaven from Asia Minor."

There is one additional fact that I simply must add. While my audience was a fun group to teach and always showed great respect as I taught, I was never certain how much was being processed. At the conclusion of our tour, the group had a share time, which included much affirmation to me as to what had been accomplished. Then they presented me with a very nice book entitled, *Ephesus: Ruins and Museum,* with many beautiful, color pictures. Each participant on the tour had written a comment to me inside the cover, thanking me for my time, my preparation, my lectures, my insights, my dedication, and even my sense of humor – which I desperately needed as I read the comment from one of the group members – "Thank you for making the twelve churches of Revelation come alive to us." I assure you I did not discover five new churches of Revelation. This book will only explore the seven mentioned in my Bible. So, let's get started.

INTRODUCTION: LETTERS TO THE SEVEN CHURCHES

Did you ever hear someone make a promise then not stick around long enough to see if they kept it? While among His disciples, Jesus promised, "*I will build My church*" (Matthew 16:18). It was to be founded upon a rock and the gates of Hell would not prevail against it. The disciples waited, and were no doubt confused and disappointed when Jesus was crucified. However, after His resurrection, Jesus stood amid the seven churches of Asia and evaluated what was being built – how His promise was being fulfilled.

This often interpreted and likewise, often misinterpreted book, is filled with:

- angels and demons
- lambs, lions, horses, and dragons
- broken seals, blown trumpets, and poured-out bowls
- malicious beasts – one from the sea with ten horns and seven heads; one from the earth with a lamb's horns and a dragon's voice
- thunder, lightning, hail, fire, blood, and smoke.

The book of Revelation is so confusing, bordering on completely unintelligible, it has become ignored by many. For them, it is simply the last book of the Bible that assures God's people of ultimate victory, and they basically stop reading, studying, teaching, preaching with Jude. For those who love the New Testament to the extent of paying minimal attention to the Old Testament, Revelation is of little interest since, according to John MacArthur, 278 of its 404 verses allude to the Old Testament.[1] For others it has become what one author called a theological "happy hunting ground" where they seek to unlock secrets known only to God.

Some so-called scholars devote much time in Revelation trying to determine the time of Jesus' return, as if that were the only message of importance in the book. The fact that the book begins with a description of *'things which must shortly take place"* (1:1), causes some to never get past the idea of setting a date for the Lord's return, when John is simply stating that Jesus is coming back. John MacArthur points out that the wording is such that it simply means that Jesus is already on His way.[2] I heard one preacher say, in typical Baptist terminology, that God had not placed him on the "Time & Place Committee" but rather on the "Preparation Committee."

I knew a man once who said he had finally discovered the secrets of Revelation and was seeking to write them in a best-selling book. I thought how amazing – after two thousand years of Christian history and hundreds, perhaps thousands of biblical scholars had failed to make those same discoveries, this man, uneducated in theological academics, had discovered the truth. The last I heard; he was still looking for a publisher for his book.

The Bible forms a complete circle. What begins in Genesis ends in Revelation. Comparing these books, Louis Talbot notes the following:

- Genesis presents a beautiful sinless Paradise; Revelation presents a still more wonderful Paradise.
- In Genesis we have the tree of life and how man was driven from it; in Revelation man is invited to eat of the tree of life.
- In Genesis we have the statement, "In the beginning God . . ." whereas in Revelation, "God . . . will dwell."
- Genesis gives the story of the first heaven and the first earth; Revelation the vision of a new heaven and a new earth.

- In Genesis, the Devil appears for the first time; in Revelation he appears for the last time.
- Genesis records the entrance into the world of sin, sorrow, and suffering, Revelation pictures the end of these things.
- In Genesis we find the first death; in Revelation there shall be no more death.
- In Genesis we have the first account of tears; in Revelation all tears shall be wiped away.
- Genesis tells of the first Adam and his dominion of all living creatures of the earth; Revelation tells of the last Adam and His sovereign rule over all things.
- In Genesis we read of the first bride, and how she became man's helpmeet; in Revelation we read of the bride of Christ, His church, and how she shall reign with Him.
- In Genesis we find the story of man's first rebellion, and of the beginning of Babel; in Revelation, the account of Babylon, and what is to be the end of that wicked system which came into being when men gathered after the flood and built the tower of Babel.
- Genesis is the book of beginning of all things; Revelation is the book of the consummation of all things.[3]

Here then is the first chapter of Revelation:

The Revelation of Jesus Christ, which God gave Him to show His servants—things which must shortly take place. And He sent and signified it by His angel to His servant John, who bore witness to the word of God, and to the testimony of Jesus Christ, to all things that he saw. Blessed is he who reads and those who hear the words of this prophecy and keep those things which are written in it; for the time is near. John, to the seven churches which are in Asia: "Grace to you and peace from Him who is and who was and who is to come, and from the seven Spirits who are before His throne, and from Jesus Christ, the faithful witness, the firstborn from the dead, and the ruler over the kings of the earth. To Him who loved us and washed us from our sins in His own blood, and has made us kings and priests to His God and Father, to

Him be glory and dominion forever and ever. Amen. Behold, He is coming with clouds, and every eye will see Him, even they who pierced Him. And all the tribes of the earth will mourn because of Him. Even so, Amen. I am the Alpha and the Omega, the Beginning and the End," says the Lord, "who is and who was and who is to come, the Almighty. I, John, both your brother and companion in the tribulation and kingdom and patience of Jesus Christ, was on the island that is called Patmos for the word of God and for the testimony of Jesus Christ. I was in the Spirit on the Lord's Day, and I heard behind me a loud voice, as of a trumpet, saying, 'I am the Alpha and the Omega, the First and the Last,' and, 'What you see, write in a book and send it to the seven churches which are in Asia: to Ephesus, to Smyrna, to Pergamos, to Thyatira, to Sardis, to Philadelphia, and to Laodicea.' Then I turned to see the voice that spoke with me. And having turned I saw seven golden lampstands, and in the midst of the seven lampstands One like the Son of Man, clothed with a garment down to the feet and girded about the chest with a golden band. His head and hair were white like wool, as white as snow, and His eyes like a flame of fire; His feet were like fine brass, as if refined in a furnace, and His voice as the sound of many waters; He had in His right hand seven stars, out of His mouth went a sharp two-edged sword, and His countenance was like the sun shining in its strength. And when I saw Him, I fell at His feet as dead. But He laid His right hand on me, saying to me, 'Do not be afraid; I am the First and the Last. I am He who lives, and was dead, and behold, I am alive forevermore. Amen. And I have the keys of Hades and of Death. Write the things which you have seen, and the things which are, and the things which will take place after this. The mystery of the seven stars which you saw in My right hand, and the seven golden lampstands: The seven stars are the angels of the seven churches, and the seven lampstands which you saw are the seven churches.'"

The beginning of the book makes it clear that this is the revelation of Jesus, not of John, even though some translations of the New Testament refer to this book as the Revelation of John. The revelation, or disclosure, was given by God to Jesus. It was then sent by an angel to John, who in turn wrote it down for the seven churches. One of the unique features of

Revelation is that it is the only book in the Bible, sent and communicated by angels.

This book is clearly *the Revelation of Jesus Christ, which God gave Him to show His servants. . . (1:1)*. The *him* in the first verse refers to John, who is only the scribe to whom the book is revealed and through whom it is to be shared. The *servants* in verse one are to receive the book and be *blessed* – the same word used in the beatitudes of Jesus in Matthew 5.

While the book of Revelation outlines itself – *"things which you have seen"* (Chapter 1); *"things which are"* (Chapters 2-3); *"things which will take place"* (Chapters 4-22) – there is much unknown, much that is rather obscure and difficult to understand. However, there is one section that is clear and relevant – the first three chapters, where John writes letters to the seven churches of Asia Minor. Furthermore, this is the only book in the Bible that pronounces a specific blessing to the one who reads, hears and keeps the words of the book – *"Blessed is he who reads and those who hear the words of this prophecy, and keep those things which are written in it"* (1:3).

John recorded what Jesus said to the churches, what had been revealed to him. The Greek word, *apokalupsis* is the English word, *apocalypse*, translated *"revelation"* (1:1) and means to unveil, or to uncover, to pull back the curtain, to remove anything that obscures or hides an object. This Greek word for *revelation* appears eighteen times in the New Testament. Thus "Revelation" is given to all of God's people, to show that which is essential and necessary.

The issues found in the seven churches are basically the same, or at least like issues found in churches of every generation. The methods used by Satan against the seven churches are the same as used today. While much has changed in the world, culturally, geographically, and politically, spiritual problems are the same. Thus, to spend time with these seven churches, exploring and praying, is indeed time well spent, and time beneficial to today's churches.

Early on, the author identifies himself as, *"I John, both your brother and companion . . ."* (Rev. 1:9a) – No claim to apostleship, etc. He does not tell us anything about his background, his family tree, the position he holds in the early church, but it is believed to be the same man who earlier, along with his brother, requested to sit at the right and left hand of Jesus in the Kingdom. He is the one who rested his head on the chest of Jesus at the Last Supper, and the one who stood by the cross when all the other disciples had departed. It is he, to whom Jesus left the care of His mother, and he who, along with Peter, was the first disciple to arrive at the open tomb on resurrection morning. According to *Foxe's Book of Martyrs*, John was the last of the twelve disciples to die.[4] Now, he is so busy with primary matters that he ignores the secondary. He simply identified himself as a disciple, a *"brother in the tribulation"* (1:9).

Where John Was — Revelation 1:9b-10a

It was this *"tribulation"* (or trouble) that got John where he was. Patmos was a penal colony, a concentration camp of sorts. Here John was shut out from those whom he loved, his supporters, his companions, those with whom he worshiped, and those to whom he preached, and he was shut in with those with whom he had least in common – exiled criminals.

The location was *"the island that is called Patmos"* (1:10) - a rocky island off the Asiatic coast, in the Aegean Sea, ten miles long and five miles wide, south of Ephesus. It was barren, void of trees and rivers. He was not there by choice, nor on a mission trip, or a prayer journey, not there on a preaching tour, or to start a new church. He was in exile for being found faithful, placed there under the emperor Domitian sometime in the mid-90s, and returned to Ephesus in 96AD under the emperor Nerva.

This was the common way for Rome to dispose of criminals. He was there because he "*bore witness to the word of God, and to the testimony of Jesus Christ, to all the things that he saw*" (1:2).

The chief feature of Patmos is the Monastery of St. John, founded in 1008. Halfway up a hill behind the monastery is a grotto known as the "Cave of the Apocalypse."[5] To this day, they show visitors this cave in a cliff overlooking the sea, where they say, John wrote Revelation.

Tour guides show an opening in the wall of the cave, where they say, John heard the *loud voice*. They even show the place where he supposedly slept with an indention on the pillow where his head lay. This caused one of our tour number to exclaim, "Just another hard-headed preacher." I've been there, seen it, but did not buy the t-shirt.

John was "*in the Spirit*" (1:10) – literally, "*came into the Spirit*" - not the normal condition, nor one that is to be repeated by all. Like that condition of:

- Isaiah (6:1) who "*saw the Lord sitting on a throne, high and lifted up*" or
- Ezekiel (1:28) who heard a voice commanding him to stand or
- Daniel (8:15-18) who was touched by an angel and stood upright.

It was "*the Lord's day*" (1:10) – This phrase occurs only here. Whether the name originated with this passage or had already become common we do not know, but it is likely that this memorial day of Jesus' resurrection had already become the chosen worship-day of the disciples. It was the day that Christ had already chosen for more than one of His resurrection appearances. It is the day that many of God's people have chosen to assemble for worship, prayer, praise, and fellowship – the first day of the week.

The vision given to John was not for him alone. He was given no monopoly of insight or blessing. The vision was for the church. John was given it for the purpose of transmitting it to others. Again, Jesus Christ is the author, so identified in all seven letters. John is the messenger. So John heard something, saw something, did something, and he wrote something.

What John Heard — Revelation 1:10b-11

Thirty-two times in Revelation, John says, *"I heard."* On *"the Lord's day"* John heard *"a loud voice, as of a trumpet"* (1:10). The trumpet was an instrument of the Scriptures:

- When God revealed Himself on Mount Sinai, the silence was broken with the sound of a loud trumpet.
- When the service of the temple began, it was with the sound of a trumpet.
- When the Year of Jubilee arrived, it was ushered in with the sound of a silver trumpet.
- When the silence of the tombs is broken and the dead in Christ rise, it will be at a trumpet sound.

But this time, the trumpet spoke, and when John turned to see the voice that was speaking to him, he saw Christ, standing amid the golden lampstands, identifying Himself, and saying, *"What you see, write in a book"* (1:11).

That *"book"* was to be sent *"to the seven churches which are in Asia."* (1:11) - Although there were seven actual churches in Asia Minor, seven is a significant number throughout the Bible, suggesting completeness:

- 7 days Noah was given to load the ark
- 7 years Jacob served for his bride
- 7 fat and lean cows seen by Pharaoh
- 7 years of plenty and 7 of want were predicted by Joseph

- 7 weeks between the resurrection and the Day of Pentecost
- 7 weeks of consecration by the priests
- 7 spirits, 7 seals, 7 trumpets, 7 bowls and 7 golden candlesticks in Revelation.

The seven churches of Revelation 2-3 were listed in logical order – the order in which a messenger would pass through, going north from Ephesus – the capital of that part of Asia Minor and the port city into which letters from Patmos would have arrived - to Smyrna, continuing north to Pergamum, turning southeast to Thyatira, continuing due south to Sardis, and turning east to Philadelphia and Laodicea, returning due west to Ephesus. (Map below is attributed to Kelly Cunningham and is available on lifehopeandtruth.com)

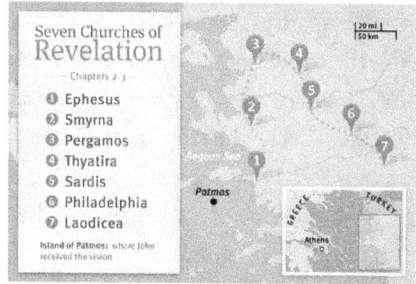

William Ramsey in his classic work, *The Letters to the Seven Churches*[6] proposed that this was a circular postal route. However, modern archaeological and historical studies have not substantiated this hypothesis. The circular route of these cities did begin in Ephesus as the letters would have arrived from the Island of Patmos into the port city of Ephesus.

Three of these seven are mentioned elsewhere in the New Testament – Thyatira, Laodicea and Ephesus.

Three are presently "living cities" – Smyrna (Izmir), Thyatira (Akhisar), and Philadelphia (Alasehir).

Present day Bergama is just to the side of ancient Pergamum. Goncali is below the hills of Laodicea. Sartmustafa is close to ancient Sardis. Ancient Ephesus is near the present city of Kusadasi.

Apparently, the entire book of Revelation was to be read at each church.

What John Saw — Revelation 1:12-16

Forty times in Revelation, John says, "*I saw*." The next few verses describe what John saw when he turned around. The words describe that which was *like* what John saw. What he saw was indescribable. Notice how many times John tells his readers that what he saw was ***like*** something.

- "*I saw seven golden lampstands*" (1:12) –This is a reference to the seven churches.
- "*One **like** the Son of Man*" (1:13) was then seen in the midst of the seven lampstands, dressed in a "*garment down to the feet*" (1:13) covering the same body that an earlier robe, gambled over by soldiers, had covered. Jesus is then described in magnificent images, derived partly from Daniel 10.
- The body was "*girded about the chest with a golden band*" (1:13) covering the same heart that earlier melted with pity and overflowed with love. The "*golden band*" describes the robe worn by the High Priest in Hebrews, and there also, Jesus is identified as our High Priest (Hebrews 4:14). Remember that John remained at the cross until the end, and thus, saw the soldiers gamble for the robe of Jesus. Now John sees Jesus wearing the full-length robe of the High Priest.
- His "*head and hair were white **like** wool*" (1:14), the same head that once wore a crown of thorns.
- His "*eyes **like** a flame of fire*" (1:14), were the same eyes that wept tears over Lazarus and over Jerusalem.
- His "*feet **like** fine brass*" were the same feet as those once pierced with nails driven through them on the cross.
- His "*voice as the sound of many waters*" (1:14) was the same voice that said, "*Come to Me, all you who labor and are heavy laden and I will give you rest*" (Matthew 11:28).
- In His "*right hand seven stars*" and "*out of His mouth went a*

INTRODUCTION: LETTERS TO THE SEVEN CHURCH... 15

sharp two-edged sword" were the same hands that were outstretched and the same mouth that said *"Come you blessed of My Father, inherit the kingdom prepared for you from the foundation of the world"*(Matthew 25:34).

- Finally, His "c*ountenance was **like** the sun shining in its strength*" and was a reference to the same as glory that blinded the disciples on the Mount of Transfiguration.

In other words, the vision was none other than Jesus Christ. John's attention was less on the lampstands, than it was on Jesus.

What John Did — Revelation 1:17-20

John said, *"When I saw Him, I fell at His feet as dead"* (1:17), however a hand was laid on him, the hand that John had last seen uplifted in the ascension, and the voice said, *"Do not be afraid"* (1:17). So personal, so intimate, so supportive! Here is a picture blending the majesty of God with the tenderness of Jesus. The touch of the hand of the risen Lord, was all John needed for that which was ahead.

John followed up with what he heard Jesus say, *"I have the keys of Hades and of Death" (1:18)* – keys are always symbols of authority, as in giving someone the key to the city. This was common use in a world of walled cities and locked gates. Jesus has the keys (and the authority) because of His victory over death.

The words used for *death,* the condition, and *Hades,* the location, are synonymous. *Hades* is also the equivalent of the Old Testament word, *Sheol,* both referring to the location of the dead.

Jesus instructed John to *"write the things you have seen"* – a reference to the previous vision experienced in this chapter. John was to write, *"the things which are"* – a reference to the church letters to follow, and *"the things that will take place after this"* – a reference to the prophetic nature of the remainder of Revelation.

Now, comes a reference to *"the angels of the seven churches."* Each of the letters were addressed to the *"angel"* of the church. The identity of these *"angels"* is one of the great problems of interpretation of Revelation. Several meanings are possible:

- The spirit or destiny of the church
- Some messenger that the church had sent to visit John on Patmos
- The "Guardian Angel" of the church
- The elder, or leading pastor of the church (many New Testament churches had several pastors). Since the meaning of the word *"angel"* is *"messenger,"* the simplest interpretation seems to be they were the pastors.

Finally, Jesus instructed John related to *"the seven lampstands"* which He identifies as *"the seven churches"* (1:20) – Jesus writes to the churches because He knows about them. Each letter begins with *"I know."*

We are often like early American slaves singing in the cotton fields – "Nobody knows the trouble I see . . ." but God knows. God knows because He walks among the lampstands and is personally acquainted with the *"angels of the seven churches"* (1:20). Pastors amid the churches – some might ask, where is God during difficulty? God is right where He has always been. He is in the midst of His people.

What John Wrote — Revelation 1:19

So, on a certain Sunday, the beloved disciple, John, was on Patmos. There, in the Spirit, John *saw seven golden lampstands; and in the middle of the lampstands . . . one like a son of man . . . and His voice was like the sound of many waters. (1:12-15)*. Identifying the figure as Jesus, John then heard, *"Write the things which you have seen . . .* (1:19).

This then is what Jesus said to the churches, as recorded by John in Revelation 2-3.

What We're Going to Do

So now, like that tour group of missionaries, we will explore the churches. There is an identifiable pattern in the letters which we will follow in each of the chapters, so we will organize our thoughts in the following acronym:

S — **Site** or city where the church is located
E – *Ecclesia* (Greek word for church) - the identification of the church.
V – **Victor** - the identification of the Lord, who was addressing the church
E – **Encouragement** offered to the church
N – **Negative** beliefs and practices and their condemnations.

C – **Counsel** of Jesus to the church
H – **Hallelujah** Factor – the awaiting reward

How do we get prayer into this book? As those missionaries did following the instruction on the churches, we will prayer-walk through them, and beyond to our own churches. After all, what was said, while directed to seven churches in Asia-minor, applies to all churches in all generations.

Therefore, at the conclusion of each of the seven churches, you will be directed to pray, after the model given in scripture, as well as to pray for your own church. To make matters as simple as possible, you will be directed to pray according to the acronym, ACTS: Adoration, Confession, Thanksgiving, and Supplication. The specific meaning of each part of the acrostic is described in my earlier book, *The Prayer-Shaped Disciple.*[7]

The "A" stands for Adoration/Praise as demonstrated in Psalm 150. This includes praising God for who God is. It centers on the nature and character of God.

To praise God is to bless God, attributing honor, and glory to the Lord. It is to speak of God's wonders while standing in awe of who God is.

The Bible is filled with experiences of praise. The children of Israel praised God for being the deliverer at the Red Sea (Exodus 15). Hannah praised God for the ability to give her Samuel (1 Samuel 2:1-10). David praised God for being good (Psalm 100, 103, 106, 107). Ezra praised God for being the deliverer from Babylon (Ezra 7:27). Paul praised God for being wise (Romans 11:33-36). The hosts of heaven praised God for being the Redeemer (Revelation 5:8-14; 7:9-12).

The "C" stands for Confession as demonstrated in such passages as Psalm 66:18-19, Isaiah 59:2, Jeremiah 5:25, Daniel 9:20, Luke 5:8, 1 John 1:9, and Hebrews 12:1-2. Confession is a perennial need and allows us to receive God's forgiveness. It is an admission of sin and the need for repentance and forgiveness. When we confess our sins, God forgives our sins, reassures us of unconditional love, and encourages us to holy living. One problem which prevents confession is a reluctance to admit to our misdeeds. A casual attitude toward sin makes confession seem unnecessary.

Confession before God is an absolute must for a believer who desires to remain in harmonious fellowship with God. The biblical evidence for this is ample. (See 1 John 1:8-10, James 5:16; Matthew 6:12; Luke 11:4 and others). Not only is confession a must, but specific confession is also commanded in scripture. Levitical law says, *"So it shall be when he becomes guilty in one of these, that he shall confess that in which he has sinned* (Leviticus 5:5)." To "sin" is a generic term covering a variety of wrong actions. To "confess" is to identify specific actions and seek forgiveness for them.

The "T" stands for Thanksgiving as demonstrated in 1 Thessalonians 5:18 and 1 Timothy 2:1. This is expressing gratitude for what God has done, is doing, and will do. Thus, we should thank God for what has been done--God saved us, sustained us, provided for us, brought us to this place, etc. Thank God for what is presently being done--God is teaching us, strengthening us, equipping us, etc. Thank God for what will be done--God will direct us, protect us, take us to Heaven, etc. Thanksgiving grows by expressing it. We may give thanks for those blessings God has given us without our asking and for those blessings we've received as a response to our prayer requests. One of the marks of Christian growth is the decrease in prayer petitions for self and the increase in thankfulness for what God has done, is doing, and will do.

The few who sincerely give thanks are represented by the one Samaritan leper who returned to thank Jesus for his healing (Luke 17:11-19). There were ten lepers who cried for mercy and ten who were healed. Ten lepers also went on their way back into the mainstream of healthy life. Only one out of ten returned to give thanks. Sad are the words of our Lord, *"Were there not ten cleansed? But where are the nine"* (Luke 17:17)? I wonder if Jesus is not still looking for the majority to express their thankfulness.

The "S" stands for Supplication/Petition/Intercession as demonstrated in Matthew 7:7-11 where Jesus encouraged the disciples to keep on asking. This grows out of a need on the part of self. Petition is that dimension of prayer which asks God for specific personal things. Intercession is that which we pray for others. From a practical perspective, this is not the prayer of a person opening heaven's doors to release God's answer; rather, it is a person opening the life door to receive answers already appropriated by God. In other words, supplication prompts God to give us what God has already set aside to give us.

The Bible is clear that we may ask for anything (Matthew 21:22; John 14:14). Just as in the human family so in the heavenly family, anything that is a concern of the child, is a concern of the loving Father. Again, as in the human family so in the divine, regardless of the prayers of the children, the loving Father responds for the good of the whole family rather than for the selfishness of one child. So, *"in everything by prayer and supplication, with thanksgiving, let your requests be made known to God"* (Philippians 4:6). While intercession is specifically prayer for others, it is included here, simply because there is no "I" in ACTS.

Having seen the background of the seven churches in Revelation, we are now ready to study the churches themselves, make application to churches of our own day, and pray accordingly. You will notice that none of these seven churches are perfect, and neither is yours.

Driving in the inner city of Atlanta, Georgia, I came across a church with its name on the front door – "The Perfect Church." I used to show the picture of this church to my Seminary students – my want-a-be ministers and missionaries.

After their laughter died down, I would tell them, do not join this church, nor accept a position on the ministerial staff. You will ruin it. The truth is, there are no perfect churches since churches are composed of imperfect people. So read, apply, and pray.

Endnotes

1. John MacArthur, *Because the Time is Near*. Chicago: Moody Publishers, 2007. p. 7.
2. John MacArthur, *Revelation 1-11, MacArthur New Testament Commentary*. Chicago: Moody, 1999, p.21.
3. Louis Talbot, *The Revelation of Jesus Christ*. Grand Rapids: Wm. B. Eerdmans Publishing Co., 1937, 11-12.
4. John Foxe, *Foxe's Book of Martyrs*. John Day, 1563, pp. 19-30.
5. Albert H. Baldinger, *Sermons on Revalation*. New York: George H. Doran Company,1924, p. 20.
6. William M. Ramsey, *Letters to the Seven Churches*. United Kingdom: Hodder and Stoughton, 1904.
7. Dan R. Crawford, *The Prayer-Shaped Disciple*. Peabody, Massachusetts: Hendrickson Publishers, Inc., 1999.

1

THE CHURCH AT EPHESUS AND BEYOND

Have you ever been in a cold church? I was in the church where missionary Lottie Moon worshipped in Penglai, China. It was December in northern China and the temperature was below freezing. There was no heat in the building. It was a cold prayer meeting. When we finished, an American asked the Chinese Pastor, "How much would it cost to heat this building?" obviously thinking of raising the money himself from his wealthy American church. "Don't want it heated" the Pastor replied. "None of the homes have heat. If the church had heat, people would come to church for the wrong reason."

That's a cold church story of another nature. The church in Revelation, located in Ephesus, was cold spiritually. I've been in a few of those too, where "many were cold, and a few were frozen!" I once preached in a church so cold, I could see the frost escaping my mouth with the words. I was in one so cold, I felt like offering the invitation for them to ice skate down the aisle.

Let's look at this cold church in Revelation 2:1-7:

To the angel of the church of Ephesus write, "These things says He who holds the seven stars in His right hand, who walks in the midst of the seven golden lampstands: 'I know your works, your labor, your patience, and that you cannot bear those who are evil. And you have tested those who say they are apostles and are not, and have found them liars; and you have persevered and have patience, and have labored for My name's sake and have not become weary. Nevertheless I have this against you, that you have left your first love. Remember therefore from where you have fallen; repent and do the first works, or else I will come to you quickly and remove your lampstand from its place—unless you repent. But this you have, that you hate the deeds of the Nicolaitans, which I also hate. He who has an ear, let him hear what the Spirit says to the churches. To him who overcomes I will give to eat from the tree of life, which is in the midst of the Paradise of God."

Ephesus was the recipient of the first of the seven letters, if for no other reason, because it was closer to the Island of Patmos than any of the other cities. A straight sail from Patmos to Ephesus would have been approximately sixty miles. In addition, it was the capital of the Roman Province, called by some, "the metropolis of Asia." So, let's look at Ephesus.

SITE — *Ephesus*

Ephesus was one of the most important and interesting cities in the empire – sometimes capital of the province and gateway to Asia and Rome. Its population was estimated to be between 250,000 and 500,000.[1]

Founded by the Greeks about 1000 B.C, Ephesus was one of the greatest seaports of the ancient world. The city was originally located on the Aegean Sea, on the west coast of Asia, now modern Turkey. Centuries of silt from the Cayster River filled in, and today Ephesus is almost five miles from the sea.

Three great roads converged in Ephesus, the main one being seventy foot wide, making it a center of Asian business and trade. In commerce and wealth, there were few cities to surpass Ephesus. It was a free city with its own governing body. It was a center of Asian justice, with the Roman Governor making regular tours of the area to try important cases. Ephesus was the home of the Panionian Games, the early equivalent of the Olympic Games. East and West met here. Cults and mysteries of the East met the philosophies of Greece and the West.

Above all of its other characteristics, Ephesus was the center of the worship of the fertility god known to the Greeks as Artemis, and known to the Romans as Diana, and house of a great temple to this goddess. The city derived much of its wealth from the manufacture and sale of images of this goddess. The third of these temples, the first being destroyed, and the second burned by fire, was the one standing during the time of John's letters and was described in the first century as one of the seven wonders of the ancient world. Obviously, paganism was strong in Ephesus.

Paul made this his headquarters for three years, staying here longer than at any other place. Much of Acts 19 tells of Paul's clash with the Ephesian idol-makers who profited from the worship of Artemis. It was to this church that Paul delivered the powerful sermon in Acts 20, warning them of the wolves that would soon threaten their flock.

In addition to Paul, Apollo preached here, and tradition says Timothy, John, and Mary, the mother of Jesus are buried here. There is a tourist site called, "Mary's House," along with the theory that John brought her to Ephesus around 80AD. There is also a tradition that says Luke died and was buried in Ephesus, however his body was later moved to Constantinople.

Even with all of this, Ephesus was the most prominent of the seven cities to whom Revelation's letters were addressed, and the strongest center of Christianity in the last years of the first century.

ECCLESIA – *To the angel (pastor) of the church in Ephesus write (2:1)*

This church, founded by Paul, was regarded as the leading church of the province. Acts 18:23-21:14 tells of Paul's three-year ministry to this church. It's possible that during these three years, the seven churches were established, since Paul's method of mission was to settle for a time in a large, central city and start churches in the surrounding smaller cities, using co-workers like Timothy and Epaphras. It was to the leadership of this church that Paul addressed a farewell speech in Acts 20:18-38. He was in Miletus, 35 miles south of Ephesus, at the time.

This church is the only church mentioned in the New Testament that received letters from two apostles. Paul wrote to this church during his Roman imprisonment, and about thirty to thirty-five years later, John wrote to this church from his prison-like exile on Patmos.

The Bible tells us that Paul taught in the great theater in Ephesus – sixty-six rows, seating 25,000 people. In fact, many other, lesser noted teachers have since taught in the ruins of this theater. In fact, if you will look in the lower left corner of the picture, you might recognize me teaching my missionary tour group.

Paul wrote First Corinthians from here, likely rehearsing it on this church. When Paul left, he left Timothy behind to supervise this new work. Later, from prison, Paul wrote a letter to this church. According to tradition, John replaced Timothy as pastor of the church here and probably wrote I John at that time. The church of St. John remains in Ephesus with its' baptistery intact. Just to prove it was real, I entered the baptistery, but there was no water, so no immersion was possible.

THE CHURCH AT EPHESUS AND BEYOND

According to Richard Bewes, this church passed all the tests with flying colors. They passed the service test – *"you . . . have labored for My name's sake."* They passed the endurance test – *"you have persevered and have patience."* They passed the doctrine test – *"you have tested those who say they are apostles and are not."* And now they had grown cold, forsaking their *first love*.[2]

VICTOR - *He who holds the seven stars in His right hand, who walks in the midst of the seven golden lampstands (2:1)*

John pictures Jesus as He *holds* the seven *stars* (angels, pastors) in His right hand and *walks* among the seven *lampstands* (churches). This identifies the position of Jesus. He is there and He observes everything about them and cares for their destiny. When churches have problems, they often wonder where God is – He is walking in their midst, just as he did in Ephesus.

ENCOURAGEMENT – *I know your works, your labor, your patience, and that you cannot bear those who are evil. And you have tested those who say they are apostles and are not, and have found them liars; and you have persevered and have patience, and have labored for My name's sake, and have not become weary. (2:2-3) But this you have, that you hate the deeds of the Nicolaitans, which I also hate. (2:6)*

Jesus knew three qualities about this church. He knew their *works*. It was a busy church with a full program calendar. They worked the works of Him who called them while it was yet day and when the night came, they still worked. Like many churches, it was a beehive of activity. We read in Acts of a riot in Ephesus brought about by those involved in the image business. So hard did this church work, that many citizens had thrown away their images of Diana, while others refused to make purchases of the image.

Likewise, Jesus knew their *labor*. The Greek word for *labor* is *kopas* and means the toil that exhausts. This church was not a place for weaklings or wimps. To the contrary, it was a working place, laboring diligently unto weariness, strenuous and exhausting labor. This is more than casual work. It is work that produces pain.

Finally, Jesus knew their *patience*. The Greek word for *patience* is *hupomone* which does not allow sitting down and passively bearing things, but rather allows a tide of troubles to sweep over it, and still bears all things. The word means to remain under; staying when the burden was heavy; holding on in the face of difficulty. Like Jesus they could have quit, but they persevered – a much needed quality in church work. Paul had to write a warning to another church not to, *"grow weary while doing good"* (Galatians 6:9) but not to this church.

Then Jesus adds *you cannot bear those who are evil*. The Gnostic teachers had gained ground in Ephesus, but not with this church. Those who came here to worship Diana had had no influence on this church. Paganism had failed to affect this church.

Paul warned them in Acts 20:29 – *"After my departure savage wolves will come in among you, not sparing the flock,"* so they did as John taught in 1 John 4:1 - *"test the spirits"* and they found them to be *liars*.

Among these *liars* were the *Nicolaitans*. Nicolas was called in Acts 6:5, *"a proselyte from Antioch."* There is much uncertainty about who these people were, but they preached that if you were saved you were permitted to continue sinning. You could preach one thing and practice another. While this group had success elsewhere, they had no success here, because they were put to the test.

Interesting to note that the Greek word for *liars* is *pseudes,* from which we get the English word, "pseudo" meaning "false." These who claimed to be apostles, were, proven by the Ephesians to be pseudo-apostles, counterfeits rather than the real thing, and Jesus encourages them for their efforts to uncover the truth.

In his book, *Unlocking the Last Days*[3], Jeff Lasseigne summarizes the encouraging aspect of this church as follows, Ephesus was a:

- serving church – *"I know your works."*
- sacrificing church – *"I know your exhaustive labors.*
- steadfast church – *"I know your patience or endurance."*

- separated church – *"I know that you have kept evil and false teachers out."*

NEGATIVE – *Nevertheless I have this against you, that you have left your first love. (2:4)*

Despite the great qualities of the church in Ephesus, they lacked one thing – they left their *first love*. Some would call them backsliders. Jesus Himself had prophesied, *"the love of many will grow cold"* (Matthew 24:12). Ephesian believers had chilled since the days when Paul lived among them, a generation ago.

First love is the love of the newlywed, but sometimes that love does not last. Simply stated for this church, the honeymoon was over. The church in Ephesus was existing on momentum, with an active church program, but had left their first love. Their pews were full, but their hearts were empty.

A tree dies from the inside out. Death is not visible for years. So it is when a heart has grown cold. Momentum carries it for a while, but not forever.

They were no longer glad when one said, *"let us go into the house of the Lord"* (Psalm 122:1). So, the bridegroom was wooing his bride back to the *first love* like Hosea did to his lost wife in Hosea 2:14-16.

Three times in Ephesians (Ephesians 1:15; 3:17-19; 6:23), Paul commends this church for their *love*. Now, approximately forty years later, it was gone.

One of my former faculty colleagues, John Newport, concluded that unfortunately, when churches become involved in defending the faith, they often lose their original spirit of love. This church then, abandoned, or forsook or let go of the love that they had at their beginning, their *first love*.[4]

Paul ended his letter to this church with a prayer for, *"all those who love our Lord Jesus Christ with incorruptible love."* (Ephesians 6:24, NASB) Thirty years or so later they had left it behind. Notice, they did not lose their first love, but rather they *left* it. It was not an accident of loss. It was an intentional departure.

COUNSEL – *Remember therefore from where you have fallen; repent and do the first works, or else I will come to you quickly and remove your lampstand from its place – unless you repent. (2:5)*

Is there hope for a church that has grown cold? There is, and Jesus offers three great imperatives to this church – *remember . . . repent. . . . do* (or if you need three words that all begin with the same letter, you can use *return*).

Jesus first appeals to memory, asking them to *remember* their past. Sometimes looking back is sinful; sometimes sensible. In a marriage going bad – remember the first love. In a family falling apart - remember the first love. The prodigal son was haunted by memories of home. It was memory that brought him back. In fact, the purpose of remembering is to lead to repentance.

Once they remember, they are called to *repent.* A church can repent only as individuals repent. A change of mind can lead to a change of direction. The outcome of repentance is action – to *do* something, in this case, *the first works.*

Do the first works, Jesus says. They needed to get back to doing the right things, the right way, for the right reason.

Should they not return, Jesus will *remove* their *lampstand.* To remove the lampstand meant the church would cease to exist. No church is secure and permanent. This church was offered revival or removal.

A letter from Bishop Ignatius of Antioch to this church at the beginning of the second Christian century indicated that this church did repent. But later it lapsed again and died. In the Middle Ages, its testimony had been obliterated. An ancient letter says a traveler to Ephesus found only three Christians there. A church lives only as it loves, and this church had left its first love.

HALLELUJAH FACTOR - *He who has an ear, let him hear what the Spirit says to the churches. To him who overcomes I will give to eat from the tree of life, which is in the midst of the Paradise of God (2:7)*

If the church at Ephesus overcomes, they will *eat from the tree of life.*

THE CHURCH AT EPHESUS AND BEYOND

This tree is first mentioned in Genesis 2:9 as one of many trees given to Adam and Eve for food and was off limits to them after their fall into sin. (Genesis 3:22-24) It is last mentioned in Revelation 22:14, where the promise is eternal life in heaven.

Alone in the desert in Bahrain, there is a tree that stands defiantly,

with its roots deep in the sand. Four hundred years old, it stands on a hill in a barren area of the Arabian Desert, and is called the "tree of life." Its source of water is unknown, and none have been able to understand how such a symbol of life can survive in such a desolate area. It is a tree one expects to see in a climate that is conducive to such vegetation. Its branches are many, extending about as far as its height. Its leaves are full of color and it is a remarkable testament to fortitude in the face of adversity. As one person said, "The reason people think it is beautiful is because it has no right to be there."[5]

The church at Ephesus, nor we, have any right to the *"tree of life"* except that the Lord offers it to His church.

He or she who has an ear, let them hear what the Spirit says to the church – at Ephesus, and beyond.

Prayer Prompters for Ephesus and Beyond

ADORATION
  1. To the One who holds the stars (pastors) in his right hand.
  2. To the One who walks among the lampstands (churches).
  3. _____

4. _____

CONFESSION
1. That we have grown cold.
2. That we have left our first love.
3. _____
4. _____
5. _____

THANKSGIVING
1. Deeds of the churches
2. Toil of the churches
3. Perseverance of the churches
4. Intolerances of the churches to evil.
5. Testing ability of the church toward false teaching.
6. For the earthly and eternal sustenance of the tree of life
7. _____
8. _____

SUPPLICATION
1. That churches would be faithful to their first love.
2. That churches would repent.
3. That churches would hate what God hates.
4. _____
5. _____

Endnotes

1. John MacArthur, *Because the Time is Near.* Chicago: Moody Publishers, 2007, p. 48.
2. Richard Bewes, *The Lamb Wins.* Scotland: Christian Focus Publications, 2017, p. 29.

3. Jeff Lasseigne, Unlocking the Last Days. Grand Rapids: Baker Books, 2011, p38.
4. John P. Newport, *The Lion and the Lamb*. Nashville: Broadman & Holman Publishers, 1986, p. 144.
5. "Tree of Life (Bahrain)" Wikipedia, The Free Encyclopedia, June 30, 2020.

2

THE CHURCH AT SMYRNA AND BEYOND

Have you ever been in a rich church - a *really rich* church? I was Interim Pastor once in a church where I had to fly to their city. After a few Sundays of picking me up and returning me to the airport, a deacon said, while driving me from the airport to the church, "From now on just get a rent car. We're rich. No need for us to be transporting you every Sunday."

I was Interim Pastor of another church that had a lengthy discussion during one business meeting as to whether to spend money to pave an adjacent gravel-covered parking lot. The discussion had hit a stalemate, so I gave them an assignment: Next Sunday morning make a list of the types of cars on the parking lot and we'll vote Sunday night. Of course, the list was BMWs Volvos, Saabs, Lexus, Cadillacs, etc. I simply asked if their neighbors drove the same type of cars (yes), I asked if they wanted to reach their neighbors. (Again, Yes). My final question was, "Would you park your car on a gravel parking lot in order to get to church?" The vote was unanimous, and we paved the parking lot – and reached the neighbors.

Rich churches are interesting. The church in Smyrna was rich, but in a different way, so stated by John in Revelation 2:8-11:

And to the angel of the church in Smyrna write, "These things says the First and the Last, who was dead, and came to life: 'I know your works, tribulation, and poverty (but you are rich); and I know the blasphemy of those who say they are Jews and are not, but are a synagogue of Satan. Do not fear any of those things which you are about to suffer. Indeed, the devil is about to throw some of you into prison, that you may be tested, and you will have tribulation ten days. Be faithful until death, and I will give you the crown of life. He who has an ear, let him hear what the Spirit says to the churches. He who overcomes shall not be hurt by the second death.'"

Remember the pattern?
S-
E-
V-
E-
N-

C-
H-

SITE — *Smyrna*

http://arcimaging.org/GeisslerRex/IzmirSmyrnaAgora20004.jpg

This city was founded by Aeolian Greeks in the 10th century B.C. It survived destruction, and was rebuilt on two occasions, once by Alexander the Great. Smyrna was called, "The City of Life," and claimed to be the birthplace of the Greek poet Homer, author of the *Iliad* and the *Odyssey*.[1]

THE CHURCH AT SMYRNA AND BEYOND

Located approximately thirty-five miles north of Ephesus, Smyrna was the "rival" city for Ephesus, although it is not mentioned in the book of Acts nor mentioned in the New Testament epistles. It would have been the next city to be visited on the postal route of the seven churches. Some would have called it the most splendid of the seven cities, named for its chief export, myrrh, an aromatic resin used in perfume that releases a beautiful scent when it is crushed, and called by various names: "the Pride of Asia," "the Crown of Asia," "the Flower of Asia," and "the Glory of Asia."

Smyrna was a strong center of the Jewish faith. Some of the hostile Jews united with the pagans to demand the death of Polycarp, bishop of Smyrna in 155 A.D.

Here the Jews built a statue to the Roman Emperor Tiberius to show their friendship with Rome. Once each year, a citizen had to burn a pinch of incense on the altar to Caesar and say, "Caesar is Lord." Smyrna Christians refused to do so.

Smyrna is the only one of the seven cities still having any importance in Asia. Today it is known by its Turkish name, Izmir, and is the 3rd largest city in Turkey, with three million in population. It is an export center for the Aegean region's products consisting of tobacco, sultana raisins, figs, marble, textiles, and leather.[2] The remains of the old city of Smyrna stands near the modern city of Izmir, making their combination one of the oldest inhabited communities in the world.[3]

https://www.flickr.com/photos/efkansinan/26310950822/

ECCLESIA – *To the angel (pastor) of the church in Symrna write (2:8)*

There is no record of the planting of this church. Perhaps it began when Paul divided the disciples in Ephesus so that all Asia would hear the gospel. Some think Paul visited Smyrna on his way to Ephesus during the 3rd missionary journey.

This is the only church in the New Testament described as *"rich."* They were poor in material matters, but rich in spiritual things, located in a very wealthy city – Jews who "knew the price of everything and the value of nothing."

This church faced great tribulation. Even to the point of death. The very name of their city spoke of death, for Smyrna means myrrh, the sweet perfume that was used in the embalming of the dead.

The Pastor, perhaps at the time this letter was written, was Polycarp.

Noted Agnostic Robert G. Ingersoll is reported to have once sarcastically said, "The church has always been willing to swap off treasures in heaven for cash on earth." Not so with this church.

VICTOR – *These things says the First and the Last, who was dead, and came to life: (2:8)*

Jesus was identified as *"the First and the Last,"* following earlier similar identities. *"Thus says the Lord of Hosts, 'I am the First and I am the Last; besides me there is no God.'"* (Isaiah 44:6) *"Listen to Me, O Jacob, and Israel, My called: I am He, I am the First, I am also the Last."* (Isaiah 48:12).

The Lord had been through what they were suffering (dead, the worst and life, the best) and had overcome. He was well qualified to comfort them and bring them assurance.

By claiming to be the first and the last, Jesus says they were bracketed, with boundaries on either side, not by Caesar, nor by Rome, but by the Lord, Himself.

We will note that each church had a specific insight into an attribute, a characteristic of God. Ephesus knew a special presence with God, as the One who held the churches and pastors in His hand and walked among them. Now Smyrna knows God as the First and Last. How do you know God? What special feature of God's character is known by your church?

THE CHURCH AT SMYRNA AND BEYOND

ENCOURAGEMENT – *I know your works, tribulation and poverty (but you are rich), and I know the blasphemy of those who say they are Jews and are not, but are a synagogue of Satan. (2:9)*

It was encouraging to these people to know that Jesus knew their circumstances. Do you know, that Jesus knows your circumstances as well? Yours are different from Smyrna but of no less concern to Jesus.

Tribulation – Some Bible translations, translate this Greek word, *thlipsis*, as *"affliction."* First century Christians would understand this word to mean they were living their lives under severe pressure, like being crushed under a heavy boulder.

In 195 B.C. a temple had been built to Rome, personified as a goddess – Dea Roma ("Rome the goddess"), thus the city had a reputation for being loyal to Rome. Christians could not participate in such loyalty. In 25 A.D. many Asian cities were competing for the coveted favor of erecting a statue to Emperor Tiberius. Smyrna won. Tiberius refused to be worshipped as a living god and allowed only one temple to be built in his honor at Smyrna. Thus, the city became a center for the cult of emperor worship –a fanatical religion that later, under such emperors as Nero (ruled A.D. 54-68) and Domitian (ruled A.D. 81-96), brought on severe persecution for the early church. Caesar worship could not be practiced by these Christians; thus they were persecuted. In fact, it was somewhat of a dangerous thing to be a Christian in Smyrna.

Poverty – Domitian had confiscated property as a means of persecution. In this wealthy and prosperous city, Christians were poor. They belonged to the lowest class of citizens. What was said about the church in Corinth, could just as easily be said of the Christians in Smyrna, *"not many wise according to the flesh, not many mighty, not many noble"* (1 Corinthians 1:26). However, when Jesus says, *"I know your . . . poverty"* He does not mean that He sees it from above. He has, in fact, walked among them, and *"though He was rich, yet for your sakes He became poor, that you through His poverty might become rich"* (2 Corinthians 8:9). Jesus understood their *poverty*. He owned nothing. He was born in a borrowed manger, taught from a borrowed boat, rode into Jerusalem on a borrowed donkey. shared the final meal with his disciples in a borrowed room, was crucified on a borrowed cross, and buried in a borrowed tomb. He understood their *poverty*.

Rich – Rich in the Lord of their church – No one with Christ is poor, no one without Christ is rich. Jesus was the richest of the rich and became the poorest of the poor – from the *"in the form of God"* to *"bondservant"* to *"death on a cross"* (Philippines 2:5-11). He understood. When someone understands me, I am rich. Jesus not only knows your circumstances, He also understands you. Interestingly, there is no other church in the New Testament described as *rich*. The church at Laodicea thought it was rich, and this church at Smyrna, was rich, only in values other than money.

Blasphemy – Blasphemy means *slander*. They were slandered by the Jews who had escaped persecution by compromise. These were not even regarded to be true Jews but were *"of the synagogue of Satan"*. They belong to the Devil. They were slandered for:

- Being cannibals – *"This is My body."*
- Orgies – Agape feasts
- Anti-family
- Politically disloyal – Refused to say, "Caesar is Lord."
- Fire lovers – End of the world in flames

And God knew all of this. Therein was their encouragement.

Jews – claimed decent from Abraham, but not *true* because they had no faith in Jesus, *"the seed of Abraham"* (Galatians 3:16, 29).

Synagogue of Satan – Here is the identification of the ultimate source of the persecution of Christians - Satan.

After all of this, one would expect John to offer words of affirmation, but the only encouraging word we have here is, *"I know."* Sometimes, it is enough to know that God knows.

NEGATIVE – There is no negative criticism for this church.

What had the Christians in Smyrna done to earn these descriptions – tribulation, affliction, poverty, blasphemy, slander? In some of the seven letters, there is a negative – that which is held against a specific church. But not here. These faithful believers in Smyrna had done absolutely nothing to deserve their conditions. They had done everything right, and were passionately faithful. Earlier, Paul had written to Timothy, *"all who desire to live godly in Christ Jesus will suffer persecution"* (2 Timothy 3:12). These Christians in Smyrna were suffering, not because of what they had done, but because of who they were.

COUNSEL – *Do not fear any of those things you are about to suffer. Indeed, the devil is about to throw some of you into prison, that you may be tested, and you will have tribulation ten days. (2:10)*

The Lord does not promise to remove their difficulties. He warns them of these difficulties. The overcoming of difficulties builds character, so He tells then not to fear. He will not likely remove your difficulties either.

Jesus said, *"In this world you will have tribulation."* (John. 15:18, 20; 16:33).

Paul wrote to Timothy, *"All who desire to live a godly life in Christ Jesus will be persecuted,"* (2 Timothy 3:12)

Paul wrote to the church at Philippi, *"It has been granted to you for the sake of Christ you should not only believe in Him but also suffer for His sake."* (Philippians 1:29).

Do not fear – Faith and fear are opposites. They cannot co-exist. Faith banishes fear. The Psalmist said, *"When I am afraid, I put my trust in You."* (Psalm 56:3)

Jesus said, *"Be not afraid, only believe."* (Mark. 5:36).

About to suffer – Indicates that the church was just entering into a long period of Roman persecution, which was introduced by Domitian and would extend to the days of Constantine (313 AD). Smyrna was known as a suffering church.

Ten days – A number indicating a brief period, not to be taken as a specific, literal period of days. It was a number symbolizing extreme, complete tribulation for an indefinite but comparatively short period of time. While Satan is free to do his deeds, he is limited.

HALLELUJAH FACTOR - *Be faithful unto death, and I will give you the crown of life. He who has an ear, let him hear what the Spirit says*

to the churches. He who overcomes shall not be hurt by the second death." (2:10-11)

This command was carried out literally by their pastor, Polycarp. On a Sabbath day, February 23, 155 (or 156, both appear in print) A.D. Polycarp, who had fled the city at the advice of his congregation, was tracked down. Rather than try to escape, he offered food and drink to his captors and asked permission to pray, which he did for two hours. As they made their way back to the city, the officer in charge begged Polycarp to recant. Brought before the authorities, Polycarp was again asked to acknowledge Caesar as Lord. His reply was, "Eighty and six years I have served Him, and He has done me no wrong; how then can I blaspheme my King who saved me?" They threatened to let the wild beast lose on him. He replied, "Bid them be brought." When they attempted to tie him to the stake, Polycarp asked not to be tied.

Polycarp Burnt.

http://images.fineartamerica.com/images-medium-large/polycarp-of-smyrna-granger.jpg

The Jews even joined with the heathens in crying out for his death. He died on Sabbath Saturday, crowds of Jews broke the Sabbath law by carrying wood for his fire. As the wind blew the flames away from his body, an angry soldier ended Polycarp's life with a sword.

The church is not advised to seek favor with the world by compromise. The ugly truth is that Christians tend to avoid suffering by compromising with the world. Sadly, many Christians do not seem to challenge and rebuke unbelievers by their integrity, purity and love and as a result the world sees nothing in their life to hate. Are we persecuted? No! The world hardly notices the church as being any different from the world – except on Sunday.

Unto death – The length of our faithfulness is to extend *"unto death."* Faithful at home and abroad. Faithful in prosperity and adversity. Faithful through the whole course of our lives. For the Sadducees, the Epicureans and the Buddhists, and many other world religions, death introduces man to nothingness -- it is the end of all things. For the faithful child of God, it is the beginning.

Crown of life – Smyrna was famous for its arena and its games. So the Smyrna Christians would not find it difficult to understand this imagery. The life of a believer would require discipline, training, energy. The pace would be fast and the going hard. There would be sweat and pain. But at the end stood He who is the first and last, the victor par excellence, and in His hand *"the crown of life"*.

A crown of victory was awarded in the athletic games of the day.

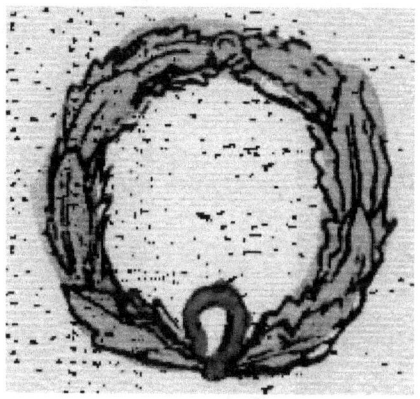

http://www.bible-history.com/sketches/ancient/crown-9-roman-galba.jpg

Diadema was a royal crown, made of leaves that soon died. Yet the Greek word here is different – *stephanos* - a crown of victory, of work well done - An undying crown of life. Nor is this the only reference to such:

. . .

"And everyone who competes for the prize is temperate in all things. Now they do it to obtain a perishable crown, but we for an imperishable crown." (1 Corinthians 9:25)

"For what is our hope, or joy, or crown of rejoicing? Is it not even you in the presence of our Lord Jesus Christ at His coming?" (1 Thessalonians 2:19).

"Finally, there is laid up for me the crown of righteousness, which the Lord, the righteous Judge, will give to me on that Day, and not to me only but also to all who have loved His appearing." (2 Timothy 4:8).

"Blessed is the man who endures temptation; for when he has been proved, he will receive the crown of life which the Lord has promised to those who love Him." (James 1:12).

"When the Chief Shepherd appears, you will receive the crown of glory that does not fade away" (1 Peter 5:4)

It provided acceptable attire for entering the presence of the King.

"Ner think the victory won, not lay your armor down. The work of faith will not be done, 'till you obtain the crown."

Second death – The first death was the natural death to which all people are subject. The second death is eternal separation from God, a reference to Hell, in contrast to the *"crown of life"* which is a reference to heaven. He who is born only once, suffers two deaths. He who is born again, in a second birth, a spiritual birth, only dies once, no *"second death."* To emphasize the point, the verse used the strongest negative in the Greek language for the word translated, *"not."*

This much we know, death will lead to a life of reward. Those who served unknown on earth, will be known in heaven. Those who never thrilled to the cheers of man on earth will hear the cheers of angels in heaven. Those who missed many of earth's blessings will be blessed by the Father in heaven. The small will be great. The overlooked will be remembered. The faithful will be crowned – by God Himself. No delegated assignment here. Reward crowns will not be distributed by an angel, not be Michael, not by Gabriel, but by Jesus, Himself, who with nail-scared hands, will place upon the heads of those *"faithful unto death"* a crown of life as a reward for their faithfulness.

A young girl from a wealthy home became a Christian during a revival meeting. Scolded by her father and ridiculed by her mother, she was given several days to either renounce her religious fanaticism or forfeit her family inheritance. When the time came for her decision, she sat at the piano and played and sang her reply:

"Jesus, I my cross have taken,
All to leave and follow Thee,
Destitute, despised, forsaken,
Thou henceforth my all shall be.
Perish every fond ambition,
All I've sought and hoped or known.
Yet how rich is my condition
God and heaven are still my own."[4]

Those who have ears, let them hear what the Spirit says to the church at Smyrna, and beyond.

Prayer Prompters for Smyrna and Beyond

ADORATION

1. To the first and the last.
2. To the resurrected Lord.
3. _____
4. _____

CONFESSION

1. That we fail to realize true wealth.
2. _____
3. _____
4. _____

THANKSGIVING

1. Tribulation
2. Blasphemy
3. Spiritual wealth
4. Unharmed by the second death
5. The promised crown of life
6. _____
7. _____

SUPPLICATION

1. That churches might endure our persecution faithfully.
2. That churches might be faithful even unto death.
3. _____
4. _____

Endnotes

1. Charles De Santo, *The Book of Revelation: A Study Manual*, Grand Rapids: Baker Book House, 1967, p. 35.
2. Joochan Kim, *Seven Churches in Asia Minor,* Korea: Okhap Publishing Company, 1999, pp. 58-59.
3. Everett C. Blake and Anna G. Edmonds, *Biblical Sites in Turkey,* Yayim Kakki, 1997.
4. "Jesus, I My Cross Have Taken." Words by Henry F. Lyte, 1825.

3

THE CHURCH AT PERGAMOS AND BEYOND

Have you ever known a church that was under attack? We have seen a cold church (Ephesus), a rich church (Smyrna). Now an attacked church.

Before my retirement from teaching at Southwestern Baptist Seminary, I felt if I went a week with no student, colleague, administrator, or supervisor attacking me for something or challenging me about something, I must not have been doing a very good job.

Given that standard of measurement, this church at Pergamos was doing a great job, for they were under heavy attack, so described in Revelation 2:12-17:

"These things says He who has the sharp two-edged sword: "I know your works, and where you dwell, where Satan's throne is. And you hold fast to My name, and did not deny My faith even in the days in which Antipas was My faithful martyr, who was killed among you, where Satan dwells. But I have a few things against you, because you have there those who hold the doctrine of Balaam, who taught Balak to put a stumbling block before the children of Israel, to eat things sacrificed to idols, and to commit sexual immorality. Thus you also have those who hold the doctrine of the Nicolaitans, which thing I hate. Repent, or else I will come to you quickly and will fight against them with the sword of My mouth. He who has an ear, let him hear what the Spirit says to the churches. To him who

overcomes I will give some of the hidden manna to eat. And I will give him a white stone, and on the stone a new name written which no one knows except him who receives it."

SITE — *Pergamos*

In the ancient world the city was known by both names – *Pergamos* and *Pergamum*. In some versions of Scripture, the city is called *Pergamum*, the neuter form of the name; in others it is called, *Pergamos*, the feminine form of the name. Dating back to the 3rd century B.C. it was at times the capital of the Roman province of Asia, but later lost its place of significance to Ephesus.

https://www.letsaegeantours.com.tr/uploads/images/202001/ber101.jpg

The word, *pergos,* means elevation, tower, or high place. The early city of Pergamos was built on a hill 1300 feet high. The hill became the site of the acropolis and chief buildings of the city. Modern day Bergama, with a population of approximately 70,000, is built on the site of the old city.[1]

Also, on the hill stood many alters to heathen deities and gods such as Zeus and Aphrodite. There were also shrines to Athena, Dionysius, and Aesculapius, the patron god of the city. It was also the headquarters for the cult of emperor worship. In these senses it was a religious center. In 29 B.C. a temple was dedicated to the Emperor Augustus and thus to Rome. The church literally dwelt under the shadows of altars to emperors and false gods.

Located about fifty-five miles due north of Smyrna, and fifteen miles from the Aegean coast, this was a frontier town – a jumping off place from Greek civilization into the territory of the Celts.

The city boasted of a great library of over 200,000 volumes (parchment rolls), second only in size to the library at Alexandria in Egypt. This library served as a center of book making. The thin, tanned animal skin used for writing gained the name, "Pergamos sheeting" or as it is now known "parchment."

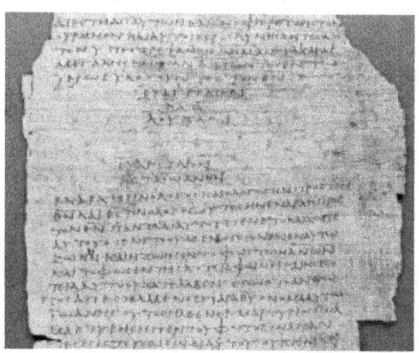

https://garycottrell.files.wordpress.com/2011/10/papyrus_75a_edited.jpg?w=300

The library was lost when Mark Anthony gave it to Cleopatra.

The historian, Pliny, called Pergamos, "by far the most famous city in Asia."

It was called by others, "Hell's Headquarters," for it appears, due to religious superstition, the antichrist was more evident in Pergamum than was Christ.

The Lord's knowledge of the churches includes their works in Ephesus, their tribulation in Smyrna, and now their environment, in *Pergamos*.

ECCLESIA – *And to the angel of the church in Pergamos write* **(2:12)**

With a major medical school located in Pergamos, this was a great place for a church of influence. It reminds me of another church I know –

located amid who knows what of Satan's junk, yet with opportunities for great influence.

It may have been begun by Paul, but more likely by one of his followers. The pastor had been Antipas, who is described as *"my faithful martyr."* Antipas may have been the first or at least the most notable of Pergamos' martyrs.[2]

Although the church remained faithful for years, it became contaminated, not by the outside forces of false gods, nor alters to false deities, but it came under attack, infiltrated by pagan influences. It did not suffer so much from the outside as it did from the inside.

VICTOR – *These things says He who has the sharp two-edged sword (2:12)*

The *two-edged sword* represents Christ's ability to protect His people even in the midst of persecution where martyrs were falling. It also symbolizes the power of the Lord's discerning judgment. He deals with error and falsehood with His Word as the standard.

Why a *sharp two-edged sword?* The symbol for the city of Pergamos was a sword. In addition, this city was living amid an intense battle of ideas, and Jesus wanted to show that He was ready for the fight.[3]

ENCOURAGEMENT – *I know your works, and where you dwell, where Satan's throne is. And you hold fast to My name, and did not deny My faith even in the days in which Antipas was My faithful martyr, who was killed among you, where Satan dwells. (2:13)*

Peter wrote to the sojourners in Asia. John writes to those who *dwell* in Pergamos. It is easier to move away from trouble than to stay put. These folks stayed and Jesus commends them for it.

Satan's throne – There were at least three reasons why Pergamos was referred to as *"satan's throne."* In the first place it was a center for Caesar worship. Second, in many temples they practiced snake worship. Chief among the snake deities was Asklepios, popularly known as the Pergamos god. A god of healing.

THE CHURCH AT PERGAMOS AND BEYOND

http://holylandarchive.com/
section_images/PergamumAsclepiusMap.jpg

This is still the symbol used by the medical profession – a serpent upon a staff. An ancient medical center, Acslepion, was in this city. The third reason this city was called *"Satan's throne"* was the fact that the headquarters for the worship of Zeus was located there, and the altar stood over the city.

Satan is not confined to Hell, as some would have us believe. Peter referred to him as *"a roaring lion, seeking whom he may devour"* (1 Peter 5:8). Jesus called Satan, *"the god of this age"* (2 Corinthians 4:4). Satan is active and, on the move, as he was in Pergamos.

You hold fast to My name – In this city most were crying "Lord, Caesar." This church insisted in calling, "Lord, Christ." Satan's presence did not dislodge the church from its loyalty to their Lord.

Did not deny My faith – They kept the truth even in the face of death. In fact, it was their faith that sustained them in the face of pagan influences. Many had bought in to the popular idea of "It doesn't matter what you believe," but it does matter. Life and eternity hinge on it.

Antipas, My faithful martyr – The legend recorded by Tertullian is that Antipas, pastor of this church, met his death by being slowly roasted to death within a bronze ox, all the while singing praises to God until his death.[4]

NEGATIVE – *But I have a few things against you, because you have there those who hold the doctrine of Balaam, who taught Balak to put a stumbling block before the children of Israel, to*

eat things sacrificed to idols, and to commit sexual immorality. (2:14)

Doctrine of Balaam – In Numbers 31:16 there is a reference to the "*council of Balaam.*" In 2 Peter 2:15 there is a reference to the "*way of Balaam.*" In Jude 11 there is a reference to the "*error of Balaam.*" Here it is the "*doctrine of Balaam.*"

Balaam was a prophet whose story is told in Numbers 22-24. Barak, the King of Moab, summoned *Balaam* to come and curse the tribes of Israel who were about to cross over the Jordan into the promise land. Every time *Balaam* opened his mouth to curse, blessing came out. So *Balaam* devised another plan – let Moabite girls seduce Israelite men by enticing them to participate in their idolatrous feasts. This would anger God to wrath. Thus, the world infiltrated the children of God.[5]

Doctrine of the Nicolaitans – What *Balaam* was to the old Israel, the *Nicolaitans* were to the new. They dared to suggest that the liberty given to us by God was a liberty to sin. They said, if you are saved for all eternity, then why not get saved then go sin. Believers in Ephesus hated the *Nicolaitans;* believers in Pergamos tolerated them.

Eat things sacrificed to idols – Here is one of the great problems faced by early Christians. When idols were sacrificed, there was usually some of the animal left over. The portion was generally served in a party-like atmosphere, and Christians were often invited. The burning question was should they partake of meat that had been offered to idols. Apparently, Christians in Pergamos were partaking.

Commit sexual immorality – In the ancient world, sexual morals were rather loose, with relationships outside of marriage being freely practiced and with very little shame. No moral stigma seemed to be attached. Again, apparently Christians were participating in these *sexual immoralities*.

COUNSEL – *Repent, or else I will come to you quickly and will fight against them with the sword of My mouth. (2:15)*

Repent or else – Christ appears here as a warrior with a warning. The Lord, with drawn sword, had halted *Baalam* in his march (Numbers 31:8; Joshua 13:22), so now he will do so again.

Come to you quickly – This is not a reference to the second coming, but to swift judgment on sin.

Sword of My mouth – Isaiah described the Lord, "*He made my mouth like a sharp sword* (Isaiah 49:2)." Paul calls the Word of God, "*the sword of the Spirit* (Ephesians 6:17)." Hebrews says the Word is "*sharper than any two-edged sword.* (Hebrews 4:12)." Jesus again makes reference to the *sword*, this time to its use, not just to its description.

HALLELUJAH FACTOR – *He who has an ear, let him hear what the Spirit says to the churches. To him who overcomes I will give some of the*
hidden manna to eat. And I will give him a white stone, and on the stone
a new name written which no one knows except him who receives it.
(2:16-17)

While there is here a warning of judgment, there is also a promise of comfort to the faithful. The Lord extends a three-fold promise to those who overcome:

Hidden manna – When the Children of Israel had no food in the wilderness, God provided manna (Exodus 16:11-15). When the need for manna passed the memory did not. A pot of manna was put into the Ark of the Covenant as a reminder of God's provision (Exodus 16:33-34).

Early in the 6th century the temple which Solomon had built was destroyed. There is a legend among rabbis that before the temple was destroyed, Jeremiah hid the manna in a cleft of Mt. Sanai and when the Messiah comes he will discover it again. For a Jew, to eat of the hidden manna is to enjoy the blessings of the messianic age. Food is always better when you wait to eat it. To those in Pergamos who refused the banquets of pagan gods, Christ will give the manna of His great banquet (John 6:47-58).

White stone – Archeologist discovered a large white stone in Pergamos with many names inscribed on it. Perhaps it was this stone to which Jesus referred.

https://i.pinimg.com/originals/a2/
f1/d1/a2f1d10c7cbb4572a12c0a42aafbda0d.jpg

There are several possible meanings. According to rabbinical tradition, jewels fell from the sky along with the manna in the wilderness. In the ancient world colored stones were used as counters for working out calculations. Thus, the believer is counted worthy.

A white stone was given to a man who had been tried and justly acquitted. He carried it as a sign that he was a free man. A white stone was given to a man who was freed from slavery and made a citizen. He carried the stone as a symbol of citizenship. A white stone was given to the winner of a race as a sign he had overcome. A white stone was given to a warrior returning from a victorious battle.[6]

In 1 Peter 2:4, Jesus is referred to as a *"living stone."*

Since the pot of manna and the white stone were both hidden behind the veil in the Holies of Holies, and seen only by the High Priest, here the overcomer is offered priestly status.

New name – In Greek there are two words for new: *Neos*, which means new in point of time – a new day, a new year, etc; *Kainos* which is new not only in time, but in quality – new Jerusalem, new song, new heavens and new earth, all things made new.

New names were always given when new quality was achieved: Abram to Abraham – Genesis 17:5; Jacob to Israel – Genesis 32:28. Isaiah hears God's promise to give Israel a new name – Isaiah 62:2. In addition, in the New Testament, we have Simon to Peter, and Levi to Matthew.

Thus the white stone, inscribed with a new name, is to be understood for its contrast with the charms worn by those who worshipped heathen gods, inscribed with names of their false deities.

The idea being, reject the appeal of the instantaneous reward, the instant gratification, the appealing temptation. Wait on God. God's hidden manna is better than Satan's fast-food fix. God's white stone is better than Satan's fancy but artificial jewelry. God's new name is better than Satan's most appealing nicknames.

He or she who has an ear, let them hear what the Spirit says to the church – at Pergamos, and beyond.

Prayer Prompters for Pergamos and Beyond

ADORATION

1. To the One who has the sharp two-edged sword.
2. _____
3. _____
4. _____

CONFESSION

1. That we tend to yield to false teaching.
2. _____
3. _____
4. _____

THANKSGIVING

1. Upheld the Name.
2. Held fast to the truth.
3. _____

4. _____

SUPPLICATION

1. That churches might maintain doctrinal purity.
2. That churches might acknowledge and avoid stumbling blocks.
3. _____
4. _____

Endnotes

1. Joochan Kim, *Seven Churches in Asia Minor*. Korea: Okhap Publishing, 1999, p. 83.
2. John P. Newport, *The Lion and the Lamb*. Nashville: Broadman & Holman Publishers, 1986, p. 149.
3. Darrell W. Johnson, *Discipleship on the Edge: An Expository Journey Through the Book of Revelation*. Vancouver, British Columbia: Regent College Publishing, 2004, p. 76.
4. Duane Edward Spencer, *The Seven Epistles of Jesus*. San Antonio: Grace Bible Press, 1967, p. 233.
5. John R.W. Stott, *What Christ Thinks of the Church*. Downers Grove, Illinois: InterVarsity Press, 1958, p. 59.
6. Ray Summers, *Worthy is the Lamb*. Nashville: Broadman Press, 1951, p. 116.

4

THE CHURCH AT THYATIRA AND BEYOND

Have you ever known of a church that was misled? How about a church that slowly let worldly teachings and doctrines creep into their congregation and lead them astray? Ephesus lost their first love; Smyrna lost their wealth; Pergamos lost their purity; Thyatira lost its direction, as explained in Revelation 2:18-29:

And to the angel of the church in Thyatira write, "These things says the Son of God, who has eyes like a flame of fire, and His feet like fine brass: I know your works, love, service, faith, and your patience; and as for your works, the last are more than the first. Nevertheless I have a few things against you, because you allow that woman Jezebel, who calls herself a prophetess, to teach and seduce My servants to commit sexual immorality and eat things sacrificed to idols. And I gave her time to repent of her sexual immorality, and she did not repent. Indeed I will cast her into a sickbed, and those who commit adultery with her into great tribulation, unless they repent of their deeds. I will kill her children with death, and all the churches shall know that I am He who searches the minds and hearts. And I will give to each one of you according to your works. Now to you I say, and to the rest in Thyatira, as many as do not have this doctrine, who have not known the depths of Satan, as they say, I will put on you no other burden. But hold fast what you have till I come. And he who overcomes, and keeps My works until the end, to him I will give power over the nations— He shall rule them with a rod of iron; They shall be dashed to pieces like the potter's vessels —as I also have received from My Father; and I will give him the morning star. He who has an ear, let him hear what the Spirit says to the churches."

SITE — *Thyatira*

From Pergamum, the northern most of the seven cities, the road turned east and then southeast to Thyatira, approximately forty miles away. Thyatira was a small city (the smallest of the seven), but an important trading point as a chief Roman highway ran through it. It was located halfway between Pergamos and Sardis on the great circular road of Asia.

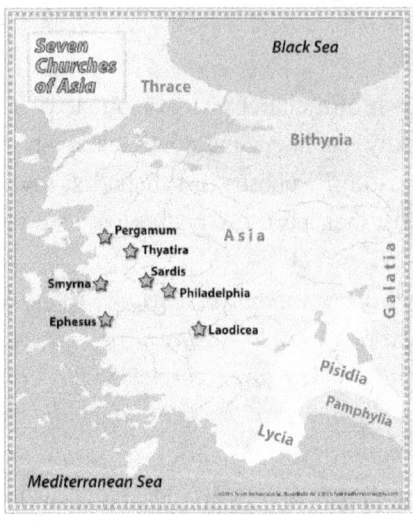

https://bleon1.files.wordpress.com/2010/05/38-seven-churches-of-asia.png

This was the longest letter and was addressed to the least important of the seven cities. So insignificant was this place that Pliny dismissed it as, "Thyatira and other unimportant communities."[1]

Thyatira was the home of Lydia, one of Paul's most notable converts. Acts 16:14 mentions that Lydia was from Thyatira. She traded materials treated with Thyatira's purple dye. She had emigrated, perhaps on business, to Philippi in Macedonia where she heard Paul preach. She believed and was baptized.

Thyatira was the home of many trade guilds, and was known for its commerce in wool, linen, apparel, dyed materials, leatherwork, and bronze work. Each of these had a connection to the Temple of Tyrimnas (or Apollo). These trade unions would collect large sums of money and give to the Temple. At the times of these gifts of money, people would celebrate by getting drunk, eat meat of the sacrifices and commit immorality with the temple prostitutes. Church members often felt pressured to attend and participate in order to keep their jobs.

This city was crowded with pagan people in whom heresy found fertile soil. It was also a military outpost, having been founded by Seleucus, one of Alexander the Great's successors.

Founded in the 3rd century B.C., this is the modern city of Akhisar. Only the ruins are left of Thyatira.

http://www.izmir.civilizationsmeeting.com/resim/Akhisar-Thyatira-Ruins%202.jpg

ECCLESIA – *And to the angel (pastor) of the church in Thyatira write . . . (2:18)*

There is no record of the origin of this church. It may have been started by (1) one of Paul's disciples from Ephesus (Acts 19:10), or (2) by Lydia (Acts 16:4), a native of this city, converted at Philippi, or (3) by some unknown believer.

The critical nature of the problems of this church cause this to be understandably the longest of the seven letters.

VICTOR – *These things says the Son of God, who has eyes like a flame of fire, and His feet are like fine brass . . . (2:18)*

Jesus is infallible as God's Son, omniscient with *"eyes like a flame of fire,"* and strong with feet like *"fine brass."*

Son of God – This name may be emphasized because here the emperor, who was the earthly form of Apollos, was thus the son of Zeus. Apollo was the sun god of Greek and Roman mythology.

"Eyes like fire . . . feet like brass" – The all-seeing vision of the Lord is further described in Revelation 19:12, *"His eyes were like a flame of fire."* A church may look good to the community and even to other churches, but with His *"feet like brass"* (Brass is strong and irresistible) He goes where no one else goes and sees beyond what others see. He treads on all evil and tramples in into nothing. This description may refer to the local statue of Apollo, which later appeared on their coins.

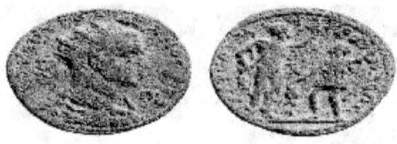

http://www.aeqvitas.com/6092LG.jpg

These coins give us clues to the kinds of gods worshipped there. The chief god was Apollo, portrayed on the coin wearing only a cloak fastened with a brooch under his chin and carrying a battle-axe over his shoulder. Another coin showed a god astride a horse ready to go to battle, attesting to the military character of the city.[2]

No matter how powerful a city is, or how evil a church becomes, Jesus is still in charge and is powerful.

ENCOURAGEMENT – *I know your works, love, service, faith, and your patience;*
and as for your works, the last are more than the first. (2:19)

Jesus knows the *works* of this church and the progress they have made as *"the last are more than the first."* So this was a good church. None of the seven churches received as much praise as did this church. In fact, if the letter ended here, Thyatira would be considered an ideal church.

Love – A virtue that was missing in Ephesus – they had left their first love, but in Thyatira, the believers still loved the Lord. He could feel it, thus He expressed his appreciation for it. Thyatira was further characterized by *service, faith, patience, works.*

Last works – They are commended for progress made in their work. Since the city was well known for its trade guilds (labor unions) Christians were in a dilemma. Connected to the guild's activities were communal meals in the temples which began and ended with sacrifices to the deity. Drinking and sexual immorality were associated with these festivities. When a Christian refused to join in, they were ostracized and boycotted. Since earning a living outside these guilds was difficult, many Christians were tempted to compromise.

What temptations do you face that tempt you to compromise to be successful? They refused to compromise.

NEGATIVE – *Nevertheless I have a few things against you, because you allow that woman Jezebel, who calls herself a prophetess, to teach and seduce My servants to commit sexual immorality and eat things sacrificed to idols. And I gave her time to repent of her sexual immorality, and she did not repent. Indeed, I will cast her into a sickbed, and those who commit adultery with her into great tribulation, unless they repent of their deeds. I will kill her children with death, and all the churches shall know that I am He who searches the minds and hearts. And I will give to each one of you according to your works. (2:20-23)*

This church was harboring one guilty of heresy (Jezebel) and spreading that heresy. The identity of Jezebel is unknown – (1) some think she was the pastor's wife, because the root of the word Jezebel is the word from which the word "wife" comes. (2) Others think this is an allegorical way of presenting the heresy. (3) Still others think she is a corrupt woman in the church who claimed some mystical revelation from God. She may be so named after the Jezebel of the Old Testament (1 Kings 16:31-33; 2 Kings 9:22), Ahab's wife who supported 850 prophets of her immoral cult and killed all of God's prophets she could find.

Dr. R.G. Lee had a very descriptive introduction of the Jezebel of the Old Testament in his classic sermon, "Payday Someday," which he preached over 1000 times. After introducing Ahab as, "The vile human toad who squatted upon the throne of his nation – the worst of Israel's kings," Lee turned his attention to Jezebel:

https://i.ytimg.com/vi/v9FnDYpIQm4/hqdefault.jpg

I introduce to you Jezebel, daughter of Ethbaal, King of Tyre (I Kings 16:31), and wife of Ahab, the King of Israel -- a king's daughter and a king's wife. Infinitely more daring and reckless was she in her wickedness than was her wicked husband. Masterful, indomitable, implacable, a devout worshiper of Baal, she hated anyone and everyone who spoke against or refused to worship her pagan god. As blunt in her wickedness and as brazen in her lewdness was she as Cleopatra, fair sorceress of the Nile. She had all the subtle and successful scheming of Lady Macbeth, all the adulterous desire and treachery of Potiphar's wife (Genesis 39:7-20), all the boldness of Mary Queen of Scots, all the cruelty of Katherine of Russia, all the devilish infamy of a Madame Pompadour, and, doubtless, all the fascination of personality of a Josephine of France. Most of that which is bad in all evil women found expression through this painted viper of Israel. She had that rich endowment of nature which a good woman ought always to dedicate to the service of her day and generation. But alas! This idolatrous daughter of an idolatrous king of an idolatrous people engaging with her maidens in worship unto Ashtoreth — the personification of the most forbidding obscenity, uncleanness, and sensuality — became the evil genius who wrought wreck, brought blight, and devised death. She was the beautiful and malicious adder coiled upon the throne of the nation.

This church tolerated one like that, seduced by her non-biblical doctrines, and overcome by their own emotions, rather than weighing her teachings in the balances of God's truth.

The Jezebel of the Old Testament met a horrible end and had been dead 2000 years, yet still her name represented evil. Even today, no little girls are named after Jezebel.

Commit sexual immorality and eat things sacrificed to idols – Whoever this Jezebel was, she led some of the believers to participate in the festivities at the Temple of Tyrimnas.

Sickbed – Thus far, this church had not yielded to the teachings of Jezebel, yet they were blindly tolerant of her teaching. Jezebel's destruction is sure along with those who follow her teaching and lifestyle. On a bed she sinned and on a bed she would suffer.

The interesting thing about this church is that the threat to their existence, came, not from the outside, but from within. It was not persecution, nor the worship of false gods, nor Caesar worship, but those inside the church who felt led to compromise their beliefs to accommodate the world.

COUNSEL *–Now to you I say and to the rest who are in Thyatira, as many as do not have this doctrine, who have not known the depths of Satan, as they say I will put on you no other burden. But hold fast what you have till I come. (2:24-25)*

Jesus will place no further burden on this church than they already bear.

"The depths of Satan" – If the Lord knows of *"the deep things of God"* (1 Corinthians 2:10) is it any wonder that He would likewise know of the deep things of Satan? The Lord seems proud that members of this church have not shrunk to the *depths* of Satan's temptations. The Nicolaitans were

the ones who claimed to know these depths, and they taunted the believers in Thyatira, who refused to believe the same things – namely that deeds done in the body did not hurt the soul. The effect was that the believer was considered above sin, and he or she could sin without it having any effect on the person sinning.[3]

False teachers, like these in Thyatira, always seem to claim to know something new and deeper about God, when Jesus says their *"deep things of God"* are nothing more than *"the depths of Satan."*

They are counseled to be loyal to what God had given them, rather than entertain Gnostic teachings – those who believed that God had given them some special knowledge which automatically made them children of God.

Hold fast – If a boat is in the water that is good. If water is in the boat, that is bad. If the church is in the world that is good. If the world is in the church . . .

Until I come – Theirs was not to be a short-lived victory, but a long, drawn out campaign. They were encouraged to remain faithful until the end.

It is unknown if this church followed the Lord's instructions. Apparently, it did not. History records that it fell to the Montanist heresy, a movement led by a false prophet. The church a Thyatira had disappeared by the end of the second century.[4]

HALLELUJAH FACTOR – *And he who overcomes, and keeps My works until the end,*
to him I will give power over the nations - 'He shall rule them with a rod of iron;
they shall be dashed to pieces like the potter's vessels' - , as I also have received from My Father: and I will give him the morning star. He who has an ear, let him hear what the Spirit says to the churches. (2:26-29)

To these overcomers, Jesus offered a two-fold promise:

- They would share in His own rule over the nations. *"Power over the nations"* was a fulfillment of Psalm 2:8, *"Ask of Me, and I will give You the nations for Your inheritance, and the*

THE CHURCH AT THYATIRA AND BEYOND

ends of the earth for Your possession." They would be allowed to *"rule them."* They were vindicated before their persecutors and promised to have authority over them. What a promise! Those who belonged to Him would eventually rule with Him.

- They would receive the *"morning star,"* representative of the Lord's guidance in the dark times of trouble and trial. The morning star usually appears at the darkest time of the night, when the night is as dark as it is going to get. When the morning star appears, even if faint, it can be known that the darkness will not survive. It is just a matter of time until the darkness disappears. If we look ahead to Revelation 22:16, Jesus describes Himself as, *"the bright and morning star."* He is giving of Himself (2 Peter 1:19), His own nature. If Christ will give to the sinner as his works deserve, He will surely give to the conqueror far beyond what His works ever could begin to deserve – His very self. He still offers Himself to the church today.

He or she who has an ear, let them hear what the Spirit says to the church – at Thyatira, and beyond.

Prayer Prompters for Thyatira and Beyond

ADORATION

1. To the Son of God.
2. _____
3. _____
4. _____

CONFESSION

1. That we have been morally impure – if not in actions, then in thoughts.

2. _____
3. _____
4. _____

THANKSGIVING

1. Deeds
2. Love
3. Faith
4. Service
5. Perspective
6. Increasing deeds
7. _____
8. _____

SUPPLICATION

1. That churches would have healthy interpersonal relationships among members.
2. That churches would be marked by the personal purity of her members.
3. That churches would hold to the faith and not be swayed by false teaching.
4. _____
5. _____
6. _____

Endnotes

1. William Barclay, *Letters to the Seven Churches.* New York & Nashville: Abingdon Press, 2002, p. 55.

2. Everett C. Blake & Anna G. Edmonds, *Biblical Sites in Turkey, Eighth Edition.* Milet, Ltd, 1997, 131.
3. Edward A. McDowell, *The Meaning and Message of the Book of Revelation.* Nashville: Broadman Press, 1951, p. 51.
4. John MacArthur, *Because the Time is Near.* Chicago: Moody Publishers, 2007, p. 77.

5

THE CHURCH AT SARDIS AND BEYOND

After more than twenty-five years of Chapel sermons as a student, then as a faculty member at Southwestern Baptist Seminary, I remember only a few of the best. The title of one was, "Dead Churches and Delayed Funerals." My first pastorate was like that –a small rural church located between DeLeon and Desdemona, Texas. When I resigned, the remaining faithful few amended my resignation to disband. The church was dead when I got there. As they say in other parts of Texas, I "funeralized" it! I gave it death with dignity! Sardis was such a church. To them, John wrote in Revelation 3:1-6.

And to the angel of the church in Sardis write, "These things says He who has the seven Spirits of God and the seven stars: 'I know your works, that you have a name that you are alive, but you are dead. Be watchful, and strengthen the things which remain, that are ready to die, for I have not found your works perfect before God. Remember therefore how you have received and heard; hold fast and repent. Therefore if you will not watch, I will come upon you as a thief, and you will not know what hour I will come upon you. You have a few names even in Sardis who have not defiled their garments; and they shall walk with Me in white, for they are worthy. He who overcomes shall be clothed in white garments, and I will not blot out his name from the Book of Life; but I will confess his name before My Father and before His angels. He who has an ear, let him hear what the Spirit says to the churches."'

SITE - *Sardis*

For many years this was the outstanding Greek city of Asia Minor. It is located about thirty-five miles southeast of Thyatira and fifty miles due east of Smyrna. Sardis was devastated by an earthquake in 17 A.D. and was rebuilt by Tiberius, but never regained its former glory.

https://www.ncregister.com/blog/are-the-seven-churches-a-map-of-church-history

Under the Romans, Sardis became an important industrial center, but had little influence in the period. It lived in the pride of its past, making the city arrogant and self-sufficient and in need of a warning from God. H.E. Dana called it, "a typical example of broken-down aristocracy."[1]

According to William Barclay, the great characteristic of Sardis was that "even on pagan lips, Sardis was a name of contempt. Its people were notoriously loose-living, notoriously pleasure and luxury loving. . . a city of decadence."[2]

Besides the temple of Artemis (4th century), a small Byzantine church, and the acropolis, recent excavations have uncovered a synagogue, the last few meters of a Roman road from Susa to Sardis, a number of shops and the gymnasium.

http://www.ancientanatolia.com/Pictures/Images01/sardis.JPG

ECCLESIA – *To the angel (pastor) of the church in Sardis write . . . (3:1)*

The church in Sardis had acquired a name for itself. Its reputation as a progressive church had spread far and wide. No false doctrine was within its fellowship. It had grown quite large. But, like the city, the church lived in the past – a past of former glory. Outward appearance was deceiving. It was a spiritual graveyard. It was filed with what we now call, "nominal Christians." No church, of the seven, except Laodicea, had declined so far in their spiritual life.

The following inscription was supposedly found on a Pastor's tombstone. It could have been written by the pastor at Sardis:
Tell my deacons when I'm dead, that they should shed no tears,
For I shall be no deader then, than they have been for years.

VICTOR – *These things says He who has the seven Spirits of God and the seven stars . . . (3:2)*

Seven Spirits of God – Jesus introduced Himself, perhaps using an idiom from Isaiah 11:2, "*The Spirit of the* LORD *shall rest upon Him, the Spirit of wisdom and understanding, the Spirit of counsel and might, the Spirit of knowledge and of the fear of the* LORD." Then again, the reference may be a reference to the fullness of the Holy Spirit, since the number *seven* is used for perfection and completion throughout Revelation. The Lord has fullness of wisdom, understanding, counsel, might, knowledge, and fear. He has the perfect destiny of the churches in His control, and He is the possessor of the Holy Spirit of God.

Seven stars – John has previously explained that the seven stars are the angels (pastors) of the seven churches.

ENCOURAGEMENT – *I know your works, that you have a name that you are alive. (3:2)...*
You have a few names even in Sardis who have not defiled their garments;
and they shall walk with Me in white, for they are worthy. (3:4)

There is so little to commend for this church that the Lord reverses the order of the letters and begins with the negative – *"But you are dead"* (3:1) – then the positive.

There had once been life. It was a part of their reputation. No longer *alive* there was no longer any need for persecution. Satan makes war against the living, not the dead. No false doctrine here – No Balaam, Nicolaitans, Jezebel. This church, once *alive* and lively, died from within. A church cannot be both dead and alive. This church was dead.

About this dead church, John R.W. Stott says, "Its works were beautiful grave clothes which were but a thin disguise for this ecclesiastical corpse."[3]

Maybe the words recorded by Isaiah 29:13 were true in Sardis – *"These people draw near with their mouths and honor Me with their lips but have removed their hearts far from me."*

Jesus called the Pharisees *"white-washed tombs"* (Matthew 6:1-6, 16-18),

http://www.ebibleteacher.com/images/whitetomb.jpg

which was a Jewish law enforced during the Passover season. If one touched a tomb they were rendered unclean, thus would be hindered in what they could do in Jerusalem during the Passover observance. So tombs were whitewashed to prevent unknown touching. Jesus might have used the same term for Sardis.

Timothy found the same true in Ephesus and Paul wrote to him about it describing the people as, *"holding a form of godliness but denying its power"* (2 Timothy 3:5).

Sardis looked alive – money, talent, attendance (maybe the largest of the seven –a 1st century mega-church). Visitors were impressed. Outward appearances are notoriously deceptive.

Still, there remained a small group of faithful saints, a foundation among whom revival and renewal could take place – *"a few names even in Sardis who have not defiled their garments."* In most dead churches, there are a few, a tiny remnant, who are holding on. In prayer and faith, they hope for better days. Even in the presence of death, these faithful followers were told that they would *"walk with Me in white."* The white garments were symbols of purity which will accompany all true believers at the final judgement. These garments stand in stark contrast to the *defiled* garments of the members of this church who had contributed to its death.

NEGATIVE – *But you are dead . . . I have not found your works perfect before God. (3:1-2)*

Dead – literally, at the point of death. It was a sickness that led to death. We would say, *"as good as dead."* There was in this church plenty of outward activity but no inward spirituality.

It was as organized as a cemetery. Few things are better organized and more dead than a cemetery. Nice trees, beautiful flowers, lush green grass, well-paved roads, etc. There is the remains of a Turkish Air Force Cemetery nearby – once organized, yet dead.

http://arf.math.metu.edu.tr/~dpierce/photos/Fethiye/Original/cemetery-original.jpg

You can't cover-up death, even though we try with flowers.

Here was the harshest criticism of any of the seven churches. It was direct and to the point – like dead men walking.

Their reputation was one of being alive, but the One with perfect knowledge said they were dead.

They did not seem to be able to finish what they started. A real warning for church starters. Their greatness belonged to the past. It would only be seen in history books.

Spiritual death in the Bible is often connected to sin as Paul expresses in Ephesians 2:1, *"dead in trespasses and sins."*

What causes a church to die? At least for this church it was a combination of (1) living on memories of the past, (2) focusing on how things are done vs. why they are done, (3) loving systems and policies more than loving God, (4) concerning themselves more with material things than with spiritual things, and (5) prioritizing care for insiders over witness to outsiders.

> **COUNSEL –***Be watchful, and strengthen the things that remain, that are ready to die . . . remember therefore how you have received and heard;*
> *hold fast and repent. Therefore, if you will not watch, I will come upon you*
> *as a thief, and you will not know what hour I come upon you. (3:2-3)*

Five imperatives: *Be watchful, Strengthen, Remember, Hold fast, Repent.*

*Be watchful (*some translations read *Wake-up* or *Awake)* – They acted as if they were asleep, unaware of their problems. Those who were still awake, were to watch. The metaphor changes from death to sleep. You can't wake up a dead man. But they were *"as dead."* Sardis had twice fallen to surprise attacks – Cyrus and Antiochus the Great.[4]

Strengthen - They were to strengthen the few things about the church that were still alive. He is calling out a robust remnant – they are in every church, a few, a tiny group, who are holding on. In prayer and faith, they hope for better days.

The faithful saints. An alive and awake minority were to recall the majority from the point of death. Every revival begins with a praying, serving minority – the faithful.

Remember – In the Greek language, the present imperative tense refers to continuous action. They were not only to return to what they first knew and practiced, they were to continue remembering and returning, or they were doomed. Memory is one of God's greatest gifts. The shortest path to repentance, renewal and revival is through memory. This was written to Ephesus also.

Hold fast - endure, hang-on. The minority group in Sardis was challenged to hold on to what they remembered from the past – former days when the congregation was alive, active, and growing. History can often motivate present endeavor.

Repent - Let an individual or a church remember what they once were, and they will repent and return. For Ephesus it was a return to their *"first love."* For Sardis - a return to what they had *received*.

I will come upon you as a thief – Failure to do these five things would cause Jesus to come in judgment like a thief in the night. They fell once to Cyrus, once to Antiochus, both in the dark of night before the residents of the city were awake and prepared to defend themselves. Now they were about to fall to God, again like *"a thief in the night."* This is not a reference to the second coming, but to judgment.

HALLELUJAH FACTOR – *He who overcomes shall be clothed in white garments, and I will not blot out his name from the Book of Life; but I will confess his name before My Father and before His angels. He who has an ear, let him hear what the Spirit says to the churches. (3:5-6)*

To the faithful in this church, the Lord promises that they will walk with Him for they are worthy.

Sardis was proud of their business in colored cloths, worn by the worldly people. In contrast God's people will be given white robes symbolic of their purity. In that day, it was considered sacrilegious to approach a deity in garments that were soiled or stained. These faithful would not have to do such. They would be walking in *"white garments."* The white robe stood for purity, joy and victory.

Because of their faith, they will have their name added to heaven's Book of Life. This term, *"book of life"* occurs numerous times in the Old Testament – Exodus 32:32, Psalm 69:28, Psalm 139:16, Daniel 12:1, Malachi 3:13. In ancient days, cities kept a register book of their citizens. When a person died, his or her name was removed from the register book. Jesus promises to never erase names of the faithful, from the *"book of life."*

In a cemetery near Sydney, Australia, dating back to 1849, is a plaque reading:

In memory of the many humble, undistinguished, unknown,
unremembered, folk buried in this cemetery, whose names
are not written in the book of history, but are written in the
Book of Life.

http://farm1.static.flickr.com/223/474163641_8eb397a455.jpg

You can have a name in history, among men, for being alive and still be dead spiritually. Your name can be on a church roll and not written in the Book of Life. Jesus told his disciples to, *"rejoice that your names are recorded in heaven."* (Luke 10:20) and the writer of Hebrews spoke of the *"church of the firstborn who are enrolled in heaven."* (Hebrews 12:23).

Their name will *"not be blotted out"* from the Book. The Greek sentence has a double negative, as if Jesus meant, *"I will never, no never, by any means blot out his name."* As someone has well said, "God did not write names in the *Book of Life* with a pencil." Far from erasing or removing the name, Jesus promises to confess it before His Father and the angels.

Way back in 1920, Bessie Porter Head wrote (re-written by David Unrau in 2007):

> O Breath of Life, come sweeping through us,
> Revive Your church with life and power;
> O Breath of Life, come cleanse, renew us
> And fit Your church to meet this hour.

He or she who has an ear, let them hear what the Spirit says to the church – at Sardis, and beyond.

Prayer Prompters for Sardis and Beyond

ADORATION

1. To He who has the seven Spirits of God and seven stars.
2. _____
3. _____
4. _____

CONFESSION

1. That we have left some tasks incomplete.

2. That we have been sleeping on the job.
3. _____
4. _____

THANKSGIVING

1. For a good name – Christians: little Christs.
2. That our name is recorded in the book of life.
3. That our name is confessed before the Father.
4. _____
5. _____

SUPPLICATION

1. That churches might strengthen that which remains.
2. That churches might finish the tasks.
3. That churches might be found as worthy walkers with the Lord.
4. _____
5. _____

Endnotes

1. H. E. Dana, *The Epistles and Apocalypse of John.* Dallas, Baptist Book Store, 1937, p 108.
2. William Barclay, *Letters to the Seven Churches.* New York and Nashville: Abingdon Press, 1957, p. 71.
3. John R.W. Stott, *What Christ Thinks of the Church.* Downers Grove: InterVarsity Press, 1958, p. 85.
4. William M. Ramsey, *Letters to the Seven Churches*, New York, Hodder and Stoughton, 1904, pp. 359ff.

6

THE CHURCH AT PHILADELPHIA AND BEYOND

Have you ever noticed inscriptions over open doors?

Over the door to the Main Building at the University of Texas: "Ye shall know the truth and the truth shall make you free."

Over the Notre Dame University football locker room: "Play like a champion today."

Over the door of a Health Center in South London, the words, "The health of the people is the highest law."

Over the frontx door of the church in Penglai, China where Lottie Moon served, is the simple inscription, "Holy Church."

Near the front door of the National Archives in Washington D.C.: "What is past is prologue."

I spent a month in Milan, Italy teaching in the churches and consulting with the missionaries. We visited the beautiful Cathedral of Milan - five centuries in the construction: fourth largest church building in the world.

http://www.brodyaga.ru/images%203p/Milan%202.jpg

There are three main doors. Inscribed over the door to the left are the words: "All that which pleases is but for the moment." Over the door on the right are inscribed the words: "All that which troubles is but for the moment." Over the center door is the inscription: "That only is important which is eternal."

The church at Philadelphia is known as the church with an open door. Over that door might well be written: "That only is important which is eternal." To this church, John wrote Revelation 3:7-13:

And to the angel of the church in Philadelphia write, "These things says He who is holy, He who is true, "He who has the key of David, He who opens and no one shuts, and shuts and no one opens: 'I know your works. See, I have set before you an open door, and no one can shut it; for you have a little strength, have kept My word, and have not denied My name. Indeed I will make those of the synagogue of Satan, who say they are Jews and are not, but lie—indeed I will make them come and worship before your feet, and to know that I have loved you. Because you have kept My command to persevere, I also will keep you from the hour of trial which shall come upon the whole world, to test those who dwell on the earth. Behold, I am coming quickly! Hold fast what you have, that no one may take your crown. He who overcomes, I will make him a pillar in the temple of My God, and he shall go out no more. I will write on him the name of My God and the name of the city of My God, the New Jerusalem, which comes down out of heaven from My God. And I will write on him My new name.' "He who has an ear, let him hear what the Spirit says to the churches."

SITE — *Philadephia*

The city dates to about 159 B.C. and is the modern city of Alasehir.

It won its name from Attalus II, whose loyalty to his brother won him the nick-name of "brother-lover."

It was located about twenty-eight miles southeast of Sardis and was perhaps the next town on the circular road for mail delivery.

Located on the river Cogamus, the landscape of this city was dominated by Mount Tmolus.

http://farm1.static.flickr.com/57/230154206_3d2e6baeb1.jpg

The district was dangerously volcanic. Earth tremors were frequent. The severe earthquake of 17 A.D. that devastated Sardis almost completely demolished Philadelphia, but was rebuilt by the Roman Emperor, Tiberius. Out of gratitude the city changed its name to Neocaesarea, meaning the new city of Caesar.

Located on the borders of Mysia, Lydia, and Phrygia, it was not only a border town, but it was also a town poised to be a missionary sending center to the east. From its beginning it was a missionary city for the propagation of Hellenism (Greek culture) throughout the land. The intention of the city's founder in the second century B.C. was to make the city a center of Greaco-Asiatic civilization and a means of spreading the Greek language and culture. Its location on one of the major roman roads made this a possibility.

This was the least distinguished of the seven cities and only a few ruins are visible today.

ECCLESIA – *To the angel (pastor) of the church in Philadelphia write (3:7)*

Only good is spoken of this church. If Jesus were to visit your church, would He come away with no criticism?

The historian Ernest Gibbon says that among the churches of Asia, Philadelphia remained erect, a column in a scene of ruins.[1]

http://www.newtestamentchristians.com/wpcontent/uploads/2013/10/philadelphia.jpg

Actually, little is known about this church, apart from these verses in Revelation. It may have been founded by Paul during his time in Ephesus (Acts 19:10). Members of this church remained faithful and strong even after the region was overrun, but finally disappeared during the fourteenth century.

Skip Heitzig, believes that this church was in revival. He writes:

This church was undergoing revival and returning to its New Testament
> roots. And as the people returned to the Lord, they gained strength. . .
> A prerequisite to revival is to say, "I am weak; I need God's strength." People in revival know they need God's power. Revival usually begins with small numbers of people who recognize they need help and who desire God's strength so much they seek Him with all their hearts.

Because of the location of its city, it was poised to spread the gospel far and wide.[2]

VICTOR – *These things says He who is holy, He who is true, He who has the key of David, He who opens and no one shuts, and shut and no one opens. (3:7)*

The Lord is "*holy and true*" as to his position; and has the "*key of*

David" as to his administration. The title, *holy* is one that God gave to Himself in Isaiah 40:25 and now Jesus takes the title for Himself. The title *true,* is the Greek word describing something that is genuine, and real.

Key of David – This refers to Isaiah 22:20-22 and 2 Kings 18:17-18 and a certain Eliakim, steward over King Hezekiah's household. He was given *"the key to the house of David"* Keys were normally held by the King himself or by someone whom he designated. Thus, the King determined who would participate in his kingdom and who would be locked out. As Eliakim was given the authority of the key in the OT, so God has entrusted Jesus with this *key*.

He *"opens and shuts"* as he exercises the affairs of the kingdom. The idea of doors is a common one in the Bible.

An open door is a door of opportunity. When a door is closed, the opportunity has passed. In scripture there is an opportunity for salvation and an opportunity for service. There was a wide-open door in Ephesus, and a half-open door in Rome. Now in Philadelphia, Jesus has opened a door.

I often shared with those who made job-related offers to me. "I never close a door that I did not open." In other words, I will explore any offer that comes from somewhere else until I discern whether it came from God or man. Has God placed any "open doors" before you lately – salvation or service doors? The only logical action to take with a door opened by God is to enter it.

ENCOURAGEMENT —

I know your works. See, I have set before you an open door, and no one can shut it, for you have a little strength, have kept My word, and have not denied My name. Indeed I will make those of the synagogue of Satan, who say they are Jews and are not, but lie – indeed I will make them come and worship before your feet, and to know that I have loved you. Because you have kept My command to persevere. I also will keep you from the hour of trial which shall come upon the whole world, to test those who dwell on the earth. (3:8-10)

Open door - The Lord gives to this church the open right-of-way to full spiritual enjoyment and opportunity for service. The door is too heavy for them to open themselves. The Lord opened it. Unless the Lord opens a door, the task on the other side is too difficult.

However, Jesus does open doors for His followers. Max Lucado reminds us that "Jesus doesn't leave us standing in the hallway or outside in the cold. He has something for us – new opportunities, new destinations, new chances to show our faith in Him"[3]

We are offered an open access to salvation – *"Therefore, having been justified by faith, we have peace with God through our Lord Jesus Christ, through whom also we have access by faith into this grace in which we stand"* (Romans 5:1-2).

Children sing this song:
"One door and only one, and yet its sides are two.
Inside and outside, on which side are you?
One door and only one, and yet its sides are two.
I'm on the inside, on which side are you?"[4]

Which side of the door are you on? This is a door so narrow that entry is accessible by only one person at a time; so narrow that that person cannot take anything with him. This door to salvation was so low that one must bow in humility to enter.

In addition to access to salvation the Lord also offers open access to the world. Some suggest this *open door* is a door to missions as indicated in 1 Corinthians 16:6, 2 Corinthians 2:12, and Colossians 4:3. Believers are not asked to walk through heavy doors, but through open doors. The mission's assignment is far too difficult unless the Lord opens doors for those who serve. We are commanded to walk through it with the Good News.

Because of the unique location of Philadelphia, this city had always understood a missionary purpose. William Ramsey believes that the city's founder, had in mind, "to make it a centre of the Graeco-asiatic civilization and a means of spreading the Greek language and manners in the eastern parts of Lydia and Phrygia. It was a missionary city from the beginning."[5]

This much we can know with complete assurance – if it is God who opens for us a door, *"no one can shut it."*

Little strength – This is not the same as saying "You are weak." Sometimes God works best through our lack of strength. So, even with their *"little strength"* they had been faithful. In other circumstances the most dangerous ones are those with *"little strength."* Some of the other churches were strong and yet not faithful.

Hour of trial - The Lord promised sustaining grace in the tribulation that was about to engulf the earth. There are multiple views of this. Some believe that this is a time of intense trouble – the great tribulation (Daniel 12:1; Joel 2:31; Mark. 13:14; II Thessalonians 2:1-12; Revelation 14:7). Believers will be raptured out before this. Some believe that believers will be taken up at the midpoint of the tribulation. According to others, *"the whole world"* refers to only non-believers – objects of God's wrath (6:10; 8:13; 11:10; 12:12; 13:8, 12, 13). This *"test"* is on non-believers. Still others believe that the church will be preserved through the tribulation, and then taken up to heaven. This much we know, in the *"hour of trial"* God will send His wrath upon unbelievers.

The synagogue of Satan – This is just a reference to the opposition – as in each previous church. Wherever a church is being effective, expect Satan to set up shop and go to work trying to discredit, and even destroy the church.

NEGATIVE —
There is nothing negative spoken about this church.
COUNSEL – *Behold, I am coming quickly! Hold fast what you have, that no one may take your crown. (3:11)*

Coming quickly – This was obviously not a reference to a soon-coming, second coming of Christ, since the idea of an open door of missionary activity would then seem useless. Apparently, it meant Jesus would come *quickly* in judgment, as he promised to do with other churches.

Hold fast – The Greek word is *krateo* – meaning to hang-on with bulldog like tenacity. It is a warning issued as the last part of the promise. Hold to His name, His word, His patience, His promise to return, and His opportunity for service.

Seems to indicate believers will still be around, not ruptured out, prior to His return.

"*That no one may take your crown*" – This is not a reference to a loss of salvation, but a loss of reward. Philadelphia was an athletic city, a location of Olympic-style games. They fully understood the meaning of the victor's crown, and what it would mean if it were taken away.

HALLELUJAH FACTOR –

He who overcomes, I will make him a pillar in the temple of My God, and he shall go out no more. I will write on him the name of My God and the name of the city of My God, the New Jerusalem, which comes down out of heaven from My God. And I will write on him My new name. He who has an ear, let him hear what the Spirit says to the churches. (3:12-13)

To those who overcome, Christ offers four rewards:

Pillar in the temple – Not "pillow" but "*pillar*" – As seen in the locations of previous churches this was earthquake territory. Remember the pillars at Sardis, just a few miles north – strong, tall, majestic, withstanding earthquakes. Often the earthquakes would destroy a city, leaving only the pillars of a building standing. Because of their faithfulness, God will make these people important parts of the sanctuary, a part that keeps the temple from falling. With the earthquake of A.D. 17, that devastated Sardis, and demolished Philadelphia, only the two pillars of Philadelphia remained.

http://www.sacred-destinations.com/turkey/images/philadelphia-columns-c-hlp.jpg

They may live in fear of earthquakes, but nothing will shake them when they stand as the pillars of heaven. They would *"Go out no more."* These believers who had fled so many times in fear of the frequent earthquakes, could not relax in the promise from Jesus that they would no longer need to rush away. Their spiritual security was secure. Pilgrims here; pillars there.

The second reward was that Christ would, *"write on him."* This represents perfect security – a brand mark. Many ancient religions used brand marks to identify their adherents. Later in Revelation, Rome is said to use this custom of branding. A faithful municipal servant or distinguished priest was sometimes honored by having a special pillar in the temple, inscribed with his name. We see evidence of this practice in Ephesus.

The third reward was that Jesus would write on them the *"name of the city of my God."* This city had had many names in history. It had been named for several emperors including Vespasian and Domitian. To have God's name written on the city provided no more glorious promise than that given to any of the seven churches.

Fourth, Jesus promises a *"new name,"* His name. Finally, ultimately, all believers will bear the name of the Lord.

He or she who has an ear, let them hear what the Spirit says to the church – at Philadelphia, and beyond.

Prayer Prompters for Philadelphia and Beyond

ADORATION

1. To the One who is holy.
2. To He who is true.
3. To He who has the key of David.
4. _____
5. _____

CONFESSION

1. For when we have misused even our "little power."
2. _____
3. _____
4. _____

THANKSGIVING

1. Open doors.
2. Power.
3. Kept word.
4. Not denied His name.
5. _____
6. _____

SUPPLICATION

1. That churches would overcome opposition.
2. That churches would be strong in the times of testing.
3. That churches would be branded with His name.
4. _____
5. _____
6. _____

Endnotes

1. Edward Gibbon, *The Decline and Fall of the Roman Empire*. Chicago: Thompson and Thomas Publishers, n.d., IV, 381.

2. Skip Heitzig, *You Can Understand the Book of Revelation.* Eugene, OR: Harvest House Publishers, 2011, p. 43.
3. Max Lucado, *Life Lessons from Revelation.* Nashville: Thomas Nelson, 2018, p. 47.
4. Songs of Praise, 1935, p.194.
5. W. M. Ramsey, *Letters to the Seven Churches*, New York, Hodder and Stoughton, 1904, pp. 391-2

7

THE CHURCH AT LAODICEA AND BEYOND

The circular mail route was ending. If a postal worker was delivering letters to seven churches, this was the last stop – Laodicea. Perhaps John had recorded his revelation from Jesus in the same order. Was there anything left to say, now that the revelation had come to the final of the seven churches? We shall see, as the letter is addressed to Laodicea in Revelation 3:14-22:

And to the angel of the church of the Laodiceans write, "These things says the Amen, the Faithful and True Witness, the Beginning of the creation of God: 'I know your works, that you are neither cold nor hot. I could wish you were cold or hot. So then, because you are lukewarm, and neither cold nor hot, I will vomit you out of My mouth.' Because you say, 'I am rich, have become wealthy, and have need of nothing'—and do not know that you are wretched, miserable, poor, blind, and naked— I counsel you to buy from Me gold refined in the fire, that you may be rich; and white garments, that you may be clothed, that the shame of your nakedness may not be revealed; and anoint your eyes with eye salve, that you may see. As many as I love, I rebuke and chasten. Therefore be zealous and repent. Behold, I stand at the door and knock. If anyone hears My voice and opens the door, I will come in to him and dine with him, and he with Me. To him who overcomes I will grant to sit with Me on My throne, as I also overcame and sat down with My Father on His throne. He who has an ear, let him hear what the Spirit says to the churches."

Site – *Laodicea*

http://www.kusadasi.net/historical/laodicea%207churches.jpg

This city was characterized by great riches. Established on the site of an earlier settlement and named after the wife of Antiochus II, King of Syria - Laodicea, whom he later divorced.

It was partially destroyed by an earthquake in 60 A.D. So rich was this city that it rejected all financial assistance from Rome following the earthquake.

Laodicea was the principal commercial and judicial city of the region, located about forty miles southeast of Philadelphia, and about six miles from Hierapolis and ten miles from Colossae, due east of Ephesus.

Three Roman roads met here making Laodicea a city of great prominence. For all of its prominence and wealth the city had a poor water supply. Thus, a six-mile long aqueduct brought water to Laodicea from the south.

Such a city was an easy victim of lethargy and self-satisfied complacency. This spirit found its way into the church.

THE CHURCH AT LAODICEA AND BEYOND

ECCLESIA – *To the angel (pastor) of the church on the Laodiceans write (3:14)*

This church had not been infected with the poison of any special sin or error, no heretics or persecutors, but it was characterized by spiritual complacency.

It is possible that the church was founded by Epaphras since Paul describes him as "*Epaphras, who is one of you*" (Colossians 4:12).

This church is mentioned four times in Colossians (2:1; 4:13, 15, 16).

Christians in the three cities of Laodicea, Colossae and Hierapolis shared a special friendship. However, the church in this city, unlike churches in other cities, was infected with no particular sin, nor had it been infiltrated by any specific heretic or persecutor. They were neither overly zealous nor theologically cold. They were *lukewarm*.

VICTOR – *These things says the Amen, the Faithful and True Witness, the Beginning of the creation of God. (3:14)*

To this church characterized by failure, Jesus identifies Himself as:

The Amen – Ray Summers explains this word came from the Hebrew to the Greek to the English without any translation. The original idea was to build up, but soon came to mean stability and certainty. When God speaks, His word is final. So be it![1]

The Bible uses this transliteration seventy-seven times, sometimes to express agreement with the Lord.

The Faithful and True Witness – Often Jesus used the word *Amen* to endorse His own comments, never using it at the end of a sentence, but at the beginning, as if to say, "This is true, listen to what I am about to say." He was the "*true witness*" having said in John 14:6, "*I am the Truth.*"

The Beginning of the creation of God – Jesus declares Himself to be the source of all creation. He has originating power and possesses the priority of existence. Paul declares in Colossians 1:15-16, "*He is the image of the invisible God, the firstborn over all creation. For by Him all things were created that are in heaven and that are on earth, visible and invisible, whether thrones or dominions or principalities or powers. All things were created through Him and for Him.*" What else would you want? Authority! As the little boy described Jesus in Sunday School – "In whom there is no whomer." He is all in all – beginning and end and everything in between.

ENCOURAGEMENT —
There is none for this church. It is the only one of the seven churches to receive zero words of encouragement. How would you like for Jesus to visit your church and have no words of encouragement to share with you?

NEGATIVE – *I know your works, that you are neither cold nor hot. I could wish you were cold or hot. So then, because you are lukewarm, and neither cold nor hot, I will vomit you out of My mouth. (3:15-16)*

Neither cold nor hot – This church was neither completely indifferent nor fervent in its zeal. They were tepid, which is the Greek meaning of the word, *chliaros*, lukewarm.

Lukewarm — Travelers coming across country to near-by Hierapolis found

http://parasolholidays.com/hierapolis1.jpg

beautiful, therapeutic springs of hot water. Stopping to quench their thirst, they were shocked to discover the water was warm, distasteful, mineral water. By the time that water had made its way over the plateau and spilled over the cliff opposite Laodicean, it had become lukewarm and tasted even worse. That six-mile-long stone aqueduct that brought water to

Laodicea from the south, carried cold water in the first mile, but by the time it reached Laodicea it was *lukewarm*.

G. Campbell Morgan described *lukewarm* as, "Lukewarmness is the worst form of all blasphemy."[2]

Laodicea resembles John Bunyan's character, Mr. Facing-Both-Ways, in *Pilgrims Progress.*

B.H Carroll supposedly described this as a man in a canoe with a lost paddle in a swift stream praying, "Good Lord, help me." "Good Devil, help me."

Likewise, it was thought that R.C. Campbell described it as someone trying to ride two horses in the opposite direction at the same time.

John said they were *neither cold nor hot . . .* but *lukewarm* and because of it He would:

Vomit – There is no real nice way to translate this metaphor. Various translations say *spew* or *spit*. It's what you do when you are expecting an ice-cold drink on a hot day and find the liquid to be lukewarm. It's what you do when you reach for the last swallow of hot coffee in the cup and find it to be lukewarm.

What Jonah was to the great fish, this church was to Jesus – a reason for regurgitation.

A person is sometimes unaware of his own body temperature, but when someone else touches them and they say, "You're burning up" or "Your hands are so cold." Likewise, a church may not be aware of its own spiritual temperature. Laodicea was not. Jesus revealed it to them.

COUNSEL – *Because you say: 'I am rich, have become wealthy, and have need of nothing' - and do not know that you are wretched, miserable, poor, blind, and naked - I counsel you to buy from Me gold refined in the fire, that you may be rich; and white garments that you may be clothed, that the shame of your nakedness may not be revealed; and anoint your eyes with eye salve, that you may see. As many as I love, I rebuke and chasten. Therefore be zealous and repent. (3:17-19)*

There were three chief businesses of the city. The Lord's counsel reflects these three businesses:

There were many banks in Laodicea, so it was a banking center for the region. They had gold and felt they needed nothing else. They were so wealthy that on one occasion the Jews in Jerusalem asked for financial assistance from the Jews in Laodicea. They had material wealth, but were spiritually poverty-stricken – *wretched, miserable and poor.* These folks would have had no trouble understanding Jesus' words, *"I counsel you to buy from Me, gold refined in the fire, that you may be rich."*

Second, Laodicea had a black wool market. They produced a black, glossy wool which was made into fine garments and was in great demand. Still, they were spiritually *naked* and needed to *clothe* themselves spiritually. However, they would have understood it when Jesus spoke of, *"white garments that you may be clothed, that the shame of your nakedness may not be revealed."*

It may be that Jesus spoke of a white garment, in contrast to the popular black cloth of Laodecia, since they were proud of the outward, black garments that covered their physical nakedness, and Jesus spoke of the inward, white garments, that could cover spiritual nakedness.

The third business was the preparing of an ointment used as a balm for the eyes. There was a medical center in Laodicea, where they produced a medicine for the eyes, made from Phrygian stone. Aristotle spoke of it as Phrygian powder. It was not an ointment but powder to be spread on the effected part of the eyes. Travelers would come here over the sand with the sun and wind beating in their eyes and find this balm to be a great relief. Yet the church was spiritually *blind* and needed spiritual *salve* for their spiritual eyes.[3]

A temple to *Men Karou*, a god of healing, was built thirteen miles north of the city. The residents of this city would have easily understood the words of Jesus, *"anoint your eyes with eye salve, that you may see."*

http://www.luthersem.edu/Ckoester/revelation/Laodicea/Men%20(Anatolian%20god)%20small.jpg

So, the Lord was ready to supply their every need – spiritual wealth, spiritual clothing, and spiritual vision.

Jesus counsels them to *buy gold . . . white garments . . . eye salve* from Him.

Here is the Good News: They were poor, but Christ had gold; they were naked, but Christ had clothes; they were blind, but Christ had eye salve.

They are to no longer trust in their banks, clothing factories, or eye powers. They are to trust Jesus. He alone can enrich their poverty, clothe their nakedness, heal their blindness. Reputably it was Augustine who said, "The saying, 'I have everything' is a terrible saying when 'everything' does not include the living God."

As many as I love, I rebuke and chasten. Therefore be zealous and repent. Rebuke means bringing conviction. *Chasten* means teaching a lesson. Jesus usually used the Greek word, *agape* – God's kind of love -

when He spoke of love. Here Jesus used the Greek word, *phileo* – brotherly love. Amazing love! Jesus not only rebukes and chastens, He expresses love like a brother to those who are recipients of these actions.

HALLELUJAH FACTOR – *Behold, I stand at the door and knock. If anyone hears My voice and opens the door, I will come in to him and dine with him, and he with Me. To him who overcomes I will grant to sit with Me on My throne. (3:20-22)*

This church had everything but Jesus. He was on the outside knocking to get in. *Behold, I stand at the door and knock* – This verse served as the inspiration for Holman Hunt's famous painting, "The Light of the World" located in St. Paul's Cathedral in London. Jesus, with lantern in hand, is standing at the door and knocking. There is no door-latch on the outside of the door. He only enters if invited.

http://d3l2rivt3pqnj2.cloudfront.net/i/prints/lg/1/0/103314.jpg

After Hunt painted his picture, he invited fellow artist to view it. One commented that there was a mistake – no doorknob on the outside. To which Hunt supposedly replied, "I did that on purpose because the door is the opening to the heart, and it can open only from the inside."[4]

He who threatened to spit them out of his mouth, now stands at their front doorstep, knocking, wanting to be admitted. Reminds us of the Song of Solomon 2:2-5: *"Hark! My beloved is knocking, 'Open to me, my sister, my love, my dove, my perfect one . . .' My Beloved put his hand to the latch, and my heart was thrilled within me. I arose to open to my Beloved."*

Dine with Him – a shared meal in the ancient Jewish world had far more significance than it has today for us. Jesus often dined with His disciples especially following the resurrection. He dined with two disciples on the road to Emmaus. He ate fish in the upper room, as well as on the shore of the Sea of Galilee with Peter, James and John. It was a symbol of affection and a foretaste of that heavenly banquet which Revelation calls, *"the marriage supper of the Lamb"* (Revelation 19:9).

I will grant to sit with Me on My throne - To the one who invited Him in, the Lord promises glory and fellowship. They will sit with Him in the heavenlies.

When we allow Jesus to enter the house of our heart, He allows us to enter the house of His Father. If we allow Jesus to sit at our table, He allows us to sit with Him at His throne.

The Greek verbs in this passage are in the present tense, meaning continuity. Jesus did not just stand and knock once. He continues to do so even to this very day.

While Jesus is addressing the church, this picture of Him knocking at the door is personal in its application. It is not the church that is invited to sit with Him in glory, but individuals, based on their response to him – that is, opening the door as He knocks.

He who has an ear, let him hear what the Spirit says to the churches. These words ended each of the seven letters. Did this church respond to the counsel of Jesus? According to Archbishop R.C. Trench, "All has perished now. He who removed the candlestick of Ephesus, has rejected Laodicea out of His mouth. The fragments of aqueducts and theatres spread over a vast extent of country tell the former magnificence of this city; but of this famous church nothing survives."[5]

He or she who has an ear, let them hear what the Spirit says to the church – at Laodicea, and beyond.

Prayer Prompters for Laodicea and Beyond

ADORATION

1. To the Amen.
2. To the faithful and true witness

3. To the beginning of the creation of God.
4. _____
5. _____

CONFESSION

1. That we have been lukewarm.
2. That we have deceived ourselves.
3. _____
4. _____

THANKSGIVING

1. Deeds.
2. He still knocks at doors.
3. _____
4. _____

SUPPLICATION

1. That churches might honestly evaluate their assets.
2. That churches will hear and follow His voice. (Hebrews 4:7).
3. _____
4. _____

Endnotes

1. Ray Summers, *Worthy is the Lamb.* Nashville: Broadman Press, 1951, p. 124.
2. G. Campbell Morgan, *A First-Century Message to Twentieth-Century Christians: Addresses Based oupon the Letters to the Seven Churches of Asia.* New York: Fleming H. Revell, 1902, p. 215.
3. Everett C. Blake & Anna G. Edmonds, *Biblical Sites in Turkey.* Yucan Yayiniari San ve Tic: Baski Printing, 1997, p. 140.
4. Skip Heitzog, *You Can Understand the Book of Revelation.* Eugene, Oregon: Harvest House Publishers, 2011, p.48.
5. R.C. Trench, *Commentary On The Epistles To The Seven Churches In Asia,* Minneapolis: Klock and Klock, 1978, pp 190-191.

CONCLUSION

As interesting and informative as it may be to study the history of the seven churches of Revelation, it is exciting and packed with possibility to consider the current application to churches today.

While God does not really need us – He has spoken through a donkey and a large fish in the past – He has chosen us. We may not be the best, but we are His best.

So in the words of Bill & Gloria Gaither:

Let the Church be the Church
Let the people rejoice
For we've settled the question
We've made our choice
Let the anthems ring out, songs of victory swell
For the church triumphant, is alive and well.[1]

Under Communist rule in the late 1980s, the churches of Czechoslovakia gathered in unmarked buildings, unable to identify it as a place of worship, even the displayed title "Church" was forbidden on the outside of the building. The harassed Christian community worshipped without any public acknowledgement of their activity. Then came November 27, 1989 – the day that Communist domination came to an end in Czechoslovakia. Churches could now put a sign on their facilities and invite people to join them. The leaders of a small Methodist church in the city of Prague, met to discuss what to put of their sign. It would not be a sign announcing victory over oppression, nor even a celebration of victory over totalitarian rule, nor even a sign displaying the church's theology. After much discussion and prayer, the leaders decided on a three-word sign. On the first morning that churches could display signs, passers-by saw a three-word sign that simply, yet boldly proclaimed – "The Lamb Wins!"[2]

Whatever else the message of the seven churches of Revelation proclaims, and no matter how much we might differ in its interpretation, and how we apply it beyond to our own churches, this much we know for certain – "The Lamb Wins!"

Endnotes

1. Bill & Gloria Gaither, *"The Church Triumphant,"* 1973.
2. Richard Bewes, *The Lamb Wins.* Scotland: Christian Focus Publications, 2017, p. 9.

APPENDIX A: HOW TO GET TO HEAVEN FROM ASIA MINOR

The glorified Christ stood amid the churches, seeing with piercing, discerning eyes, complementing the positives, identifying negative characteristics, and offering wise counsel. This message, delivered first to the seven churches of Asia, is universal. Its truth applies wherever similar conditions are found today.

Even as John's vision had Jesus walking on the Roman roads of the seven cities of Asia Minor, so there is a road, recorded in Romans, that if followed, leads one to Jesus. Consider then, the Roman Road to Salvation:

1. The Bible affirms God loves you and demonstrated that love through His Son, Jesus Christ. *"God demonstrates His own love toward us, in that while we were still sinners, Christ died for us."* (Romans 5:8) See also John 3:16; John 10:10; John 17:24.
2. The reason Christ died is because mankind was sinful. *"All have sinned and fall short of the glory of God."* (Romans 3:23). See also Isaiah 53:6; Isaiah 59:2; 2 Chronicles 6:36.
3. So, because of the sinfulness of mankind, God allowed His only son to die. *"Who was delivered up because of our offenses, and was raised because of our justification."*

(Romans 4:25). See also Isaiah 53:5; John 4:16; John 14:6; Ephesians 1:7.
4. If Jesus Christ had not died for our sin, we would have to die in our sin. *"For the wages of sin is death, but the gift of God is eternal life in Christ Jesus our Lord."* (Romans 6:23). See also John 11:25-26.
5. So great was God's love and Christ's sacrifice, that we must respond in repentance, confession and faith. *"If you confess with your mouth the Lord Jesus and believe in your heart that God has raised Him from the dead, you will be saved."* (Romans 10:9). See also Isaiah 55:6; Mark 1:15; John 1:12; I John 1:9.
6. So what is your decision? To the church at Laodicea, John wrote these words of Jesus: *"Behold, I stand at the door and knock. If anyone hears My voice and opens the door, I will come in to him and dine with him, and he with Me."* (Revelation 3:20). In response to the question, *"What must I do to be saved?"* Paul replied, *"Believe on the Lord Jesus Christ, and you will be saved, you and your household."* (Acts 16:30-31).
7. If you understand what God did for you, your decision needs to be made today. *"In an acceptable time I have heard you, and in the day of salvation I have helped you. Behold, now is the accepted time; behold, now is the day of salvation."* (2 Corinthians 6:2). *"Today, if you will hear His voice, do not harden your hearts."* (Hebrews 4:7). *"The Scriptures tell us that no one who believes in Christ will ever be disappointed."* (Romans 10:10, TLB)

With Revelation 4 we turn from the Church on earth to the Church in heaven, from Christ among the flickering lampstands to Christ near the unchangeable throne of God. (Revelation 4:1-2) If you have not yet guaranteed your place around that eternal throne, please consider doing so today.

He that has an ear, let him hear.

BIBLIOGRAPHY

Allen, Cady H. *The Message of the Book of Revelation.* New York/Nashville: Abingdon-Cokesbury Press, 1939.

Baldinger, Albert H, *Sermons on Revelation.* New York: George H. Doran Company, 1924.

Barclay, William, *Letters to the Seven Churches.* New York/Nashville: Abingdon Press, 1957.

Bewes, Richard, *The Lamb Wins: A Guided Tour Through the Book of Revelation.* Scotland: Christian Focus Publications, 2017.

Blake, Everett C. & Anna G. Edmonds, *Biblical Sites in Turkey.* Milet, Ltd, 2002.

Chappell, Clovis G, *Sermons from Revelation.* New York/Nashville: Abingdon-Cokesbury Press, 1953.

De Santo, Charles, *The Book of Revelation: A Study Manual,* Grand Rapids: Baker Book House, 1967.

Farrer, Austin, *The Revelation of St. John the Divine.* Oxford: Clarendon Press, 1964.

Grant, J. Ralph, *Letters to the Seven Churches.* Grand Rapids: Baker Book House, 1962.

BIBLIOGRAPHY

Heitzig, Skip, *You Can Understand the Book of Revelation*. Eugene: Harvest House Publishers, 2011.

Hemer, Colin J., *The Letters to the Seven Churches of Asia in Their Local Setting*. Grand Rapids: Eerdmans, 2001.

Jeremiah, David, *The Seven Churches of Revelation Study Guide*. Turning Point, 2016.

Johnson, Darrell W., *Discipleship on the Edge: An Expository Journey through the Book of Revelation*. Vancouver, British Columbia, Canada: Regent College Publishing, 2004.

Kim, Joochan. *Seven Churches in Asia Minor*. Korea: Okhap Publishing, 1999.

LaHaye, Tim and Parker, Timothy E. *The Book of Revelation Made Clear*. Nashville: Thomas Nelson, Inc., 2014.

Lasseigne, Jeff, *Unlocking the Last Days*. Grand Rapids: Baker Books, 2011.

Lawrence, J.B., *A New Heaven and a New Earth*. New York: American Press Publications, Inc., 1960.

Lucado, Max, *Life Lessons from Revelation*. Nashville: Thomas Nelson, Inc., 2017.

MacArthur, John, *Because the Time is Near*. Chicago: Moody Publishers, 2007.

McDowell, Edward A. *The Meaning and Message of the Book of Revelation*. Nashville: Broadman Press, 1951.

Morgan, G. Campbell. *A First-Century Message to Twentieth-Century Christians: Addresses Based oupon the Letters to the Seven Churches of Asia*. New York: Fleming H. Revell, 1902.

Newport, John P. *The Lion and the Lamb*. Nashville: Broadman & Holman Publishers, 1986.

Palmer, Chris, *Letters from Jesus: Studies from the Seven Churches of Revelation*. New Kensington, PA, 2019.

Ramsey, William M, *Letters to the Seven Churches*. United Kingdom: Hodder and Stoughton, 1904.

Spencer, Duane Edward, *The Seven Epistles of Jesus*. San Antonio: Grace Bible Press, 1967.

Spilsbury, Paul, *The Throne, The Lamb, The Dragon*. Downers Grove, ILL: Inter-Varsity Press, 2002.

Stott, John R.W. *What Christ Thinks of the Church: An Exposition of Revelation 2-3.* Grand Rapids: Baker Publishing Group, 2003.

Summers, Ray, *Worthy is the Lamb.* Nashville: Broadman Press, 1951.

Talbot, Louis T. *The Revelation of Jesus Christ.* Grand Rapids: Wm. B. Eerdmans Publishing Co., 1937.

Trench, R.C., *Commentary on the Epistles to the Seven Churches in Asia.* Minneapolis: Klock and Klock, 1978.

Welton, Jonathan, *Understanding the Seven Churches of Revelation.* Rochester, NY: Welton Academy, 2015